Extreme Students

Challenging All Students and Energizing Learning

Keen J. Babbage

Rowman & Littlefield Education
Lanham, Maryland • Toronto • Oxford
2006

Published in the United States of America
by Rowman & Littlefield Education
A Division of Rowman & Littlefield Publishers, Inc.
A wholly owned subsidary of The Rowman & Littlefield Publishing Group, Inc.
4501 Forbes Boulevard, Suite 200, Lanham, Maryland 20706
www.rowmaneducation.com

PO Box 317
Oxford
OX2 9RU, UK

British Library Cataloguing in Publication Information Available

Library of Congress Cataloging-in-Publication Data

Babbage, Keen J.
  Extreme students : challenging all students and energizing
learning / Keen J. Babbage.
      p. cm.
  Includes index.
  ISBN 1-57886-312-0 (pbk. : alk. paper)
  1. Motivation in education. 2. Learning. 3. Academic
achievement. I. Title.

  LB1065.B228 2005
  370.15'4—dc22

                                        2005014500

∞^{TM} The paper used in this publication meets the minimum requirements of
American National Standard for Information Sciences—Permanence of Paper
for Printed Library Materials, ANSI/NISO Z39.48-1992.
Manufactured in the United States of America.

Dedicated to my students—
past, present, and future

Contents

Preface

I began teaching in 1980. I promised myself to use vibrant teaching methods, have lively class discussions, have varied classroom activities, have genuine interaction with students, and create demanding tests. The results at three different schools were that most students made good grades, but not all students. Most students committed to my classes and most parents and guardians appreciated the good experiences.

I began extreme teaching in the 2000–2001 school year, and the results were better—extremely better. This is the fourth school where I have worked. I am in my twenty-first year of teaching and administration. What caused me to change my teaching methods from being merely vibrant, lively, varied, interactive, genuine, and demanding to be extremely vibrant, lively, varied, interactive, genuine, and demanding? The principal of my school asked me, the assistant principal, if I would like to teach a seventh grade critical thinking class. My "yes, sir" was immediate and did not waver when he told me that the school had no materials for the class. My silent thought was, "Rejoice and give thanks. The students and I get to invent the class and create the activities." Without the restrictions of required materials, the critical thinking activities had no boundaries, no limits, no rules of conformity, and no routine.

I discovered that the most powerful and productive resource was the wholesome knowledge, interests, and talents of the students. Their knowledge of basketball led us to sophisticated mathematical analysis of basketball statistics. Their interest in money inspired our creation of new products and the marketing programs to advertise and promote the products. Their talents in creative writing were applied when each student designed and produced a magazine with topics ranging from fashions to roller coasters.

It became apparent that any part of the school's curriculum, the school district's curriculum guidelines, and the state's curriculum/core content could be mastered through creative classroom activities that connected the wholesome knowledge, interests, and talents of students with what students needed to learn.

That insight was tested and confirmed when my teaching adventure changed from critical thinking to world history and then economics. There were endless possibilities for making meaningful academic learning connections between the wholesome knowledge, interests, and talents of students and what they needed to learn. Students created a candy bar designed to have been sold at the height of the Roman Empire. The students' knowledge of and interest in candy connected with details of the Roman Empire to create learning and inspire commitment. Students created new brands of breakfast cereal to master essential concepts of and vocabulary in economics. These ideas and methods are fully explained in *Extreme Teaching* and *Extreme Learning*.

The human brain is eager to make connections. Students bring wholesome knowledge, interests, and talents to school with them. Teachers seek ways to motivate each student to succeed at school. My research and teaching experience confirm that extreme teaching results in extreme learning. My experience also shows that students respond enthusiastically to extreme teaching and eagerly experience extreme learning for many reasons, including these:

1. School becomes real when learning at school connects with the knowledge, interests, and talents of students.
2. There is no "why do we have to learn this" or "when will we ever need this" when learning at school is real, because it connects with students' interests.
3. As students see that their life experience and input become essential classroom resources, they are more likely to team up with a teacher to create a mutually beneficial classroom learning community.
4. Grades are good, students succeed academically, and achievement gaps can be reduced or eliminated. In the past three years all students in my extreme teaching and extreme learning economics classes have made an A or B grade. The more extreme the teaching is the more extreme the learning is.
5. Outstanding students have expanded their skills through the unique extreme learning experiences, which required new thinking and new work by those students for whom school can sometimes present few challenges.
6. Students who were not accustomed to making A or B grades responded to the extreme teaching and extreme learning experiences by making an A or a B.

Extreme Learning was written because I underestimated the *Extreme Teaching* impact on creating a learning community. I knew that the *Extreme Teaching* methods would cause learning. I realized that this learning was extreme because of the authentic partnership, teamwork, and learning community created as teacher and students learn with each other and from each other. There was more. Great students were stretching themselves into new levels of academic achievements, and students who had not yet seen themselves as great students were now doing outstanding work. Some students who had been comfortable for years with C averages were discovering that they could do the work to make an A or B grade, that they could willingly do all homework, and that they could participate in class discussions with important contributions.

The students were becoming extreme students. They were eager and willing to accept their responsibility to learn, learn more, and keep learning. The students motivated me. The teacher motivated the students. The teaching fascinated everyone as we learned from each other and with each other. An extreme teacher and a classroom of extreme students were causing extreme learning.

How did these young scholars become extreme students who were eager to learn, learn more, and keep learning? What is it about extreme teaching and extreme learning that inspires, convinces, nurtures, justifies, and creates extreme students? The research done for this book helps answer those questions. My recent experiences with eighth graders who became extreme students personalize that research. When knowledge is personal it is real, and when it is real it can be applied in many places.

In the past two years, 93 percent of my students earned an A grade and 7 percent earned a B grade. There was no achievement gap. The more extreme my teaching is, the more extreme the learning is. My career has been in middle school and high school with part-time college or graduate school teaching. Elementary schoolteachers I have taught in graduate school classes confirm that the extreme teaching approach is effective for them and their students. My personal career experience does not include elementary school.

Students are real people living real lives right now. Teachers are real people doing real work right now. When the real-life experience of students is connected by skillful teachers to what needs to be learned at school, the results are symbiotic, productive, and meaningful. Still, more can be done and this book is designed to show how. The ideas in this book are intended to provide real insights and methods to create, nurture, and inspire extreme teaching, extreme learning, and extreme students.

Acknowledgments

Students I have taught in middle school, high school, and college and graduate school classes are the people with whom and for whom the extreme teaching method was designed. Their willingness to go where their brain had not gone before, learn in a dynamic and unpredictable process, and team up with me to create a classroom learning community have been a blessing to me. To learn with and from students is a real joy.

My family is always patient, understanding, and encouraging while I write a book. I appreciate their kind tolerance of my no to certain requests so I can say yes to a book that is asking to be written now.

My parents and my grandparents insisted that I do well at school. They also reared me with experiences that supported my curiosity and expanded my wholesome knowledge, interests, and talents. Through their extreme teaching they made me an extreme student who sought and still seeks extreme learning.

Dr. Earl Reum taught hundreds of thousands of middle school and high school students about leadership. In the 1970s I attended many weeklong leadership workshops that Dr. Reum organized and taught. His teaching always captivated the students. I asked myself, "Can't this type of great teaching happen in classrooms just as it does at these summer workshops?" My conclusion was that the classroom could match the summer workshop. Dr. Reum inspired me to set that standard for my teaching.

Dr. Larry Matheny has convinced thousands of students at Centre College in Danville, Kentucky, that political philosophy merits total attention and complete commitment. Dr. Matheny is the only professor I have known whose classes sometimes attracted students who were not taking the class; they knew that certain of his lectures/discussions were essential for an educated person. After his classes some of the students would discuss Plato, Aristotle, and other political philosophers for hours. Dr. Matheny inspired us to be extreme students.

Cindy Henderson is a computer expert who transforms my rough handwriting into a clean manuscript. I write manuscripts by hand because it works for me. Cindy's computer skills have enhanced every manuscript of mine. She, her husband, and their three children have encouraged me through six book adventures. Their friendship is one of the important benefits I have obtained through a decade of writing six books.

Jim Thomas, the principal of Bryan Station Middle School in Lexington, Kentucky, allowed me to teach one class each year for the past five years. That increases his workload, but he knows that the students benefit and that I thrive in the classroom. No matter what difficulties challenge me daily as assistant principal, they never erase the joys of teaching a class daily.

My grandfather, Keen Johnson, was governor of Kentucky from 1939 to 1943. Education was a high priority for Governor Johnson. His father had insisted that he go to college, and he credited this success in life to the foundation his parents provided. I attribute similar credit to my grandparents and to my parents. My mother, Judy Babbage, is the daughter of Keen and Eunice Johnson. Mother was the first female student at the University of Kentucky to make straight A grades in every class for four years of college. She earned Phi Beta Kappa membership. My heritage is one of extreme teaching and extreme learning creating extreme students. My brother and sister-in-law, Bob and Laura, are rearing three impressive, extreme students—Robert, Julie, and Brian—who continue the family tradition of learn, learn more, and keep learning.

From 1976 to 1980 I worked in advertising for Procter & Gamble. The impact of my teaching is doubled or tripled because of the work ethic and work standards Procter & Gamble taught me. I answered a question asked by my first boss at Procter & Gamble in the summer of 1976. Her reply was, "That's unacceptable." I found an acceptable answer quickly. I am convinced that we know what works in education; therefore, failure is unacceptable and doing what does not work is unacceptable.

The students in our classrooms can become extreme students who experience and seek extreme learning when challenged and inspired by extreme teaching. I thank the people who have convinced me of this truth.

Introduction

There is no inherent limit to human thought. The brain is ready, willing, and able to think at all times. The mind is eager to analyze, reflect, and understand at all times. The human body has physical limitations. Running a mile in four minutes was once seen as impossible but is now common among the greatest runners; however, there is no expectation that a superior runner will run a mile in under three minutes. We can think about a three-minute mile even though no human can currently run a mile that quickly. There is no inherent limit to human thought.

Some limitations are placed on thinking, but these can be removed. One such limitation in school is the regularized routine of ordinary classroom activities. Textbooks, worksheets, and videos followed by tests on Friday result in limited learning and do not inspire a student's eagerness to vibrantly learn, think, know, wonder, explore, research, analyze, and reflect. They also limit the career experiences of teachers.

To expand thinking to the extreme requires teaching and learning experiences that are infinite rather than the rigidly finite routine of textbooks, worksheets, videos, and tests on Friday.

In recent years educators have been asked to expand the skill levels of students to include mastery of critical thinking and problem solving. That can be done, but not with longer textbooks, more worksheets, longer videos, and longer tests on Friday. Those teaching and learning methods are severely limited in the results they can impact. To inspire students and nurture an eagerness to master all academic basics and advanced intellectual skills requires classroom teaching and learning experiences that cause mastery to occur. Getting different, better results can happen by using different, better teaching and learning methods.

Textbooks or worksheets presented on a computer screen are still textbooks and worksheets. There are useful instructional technologies that can enhance teaching and learning; however, a limited, superficial worksheet does not magically become a brain-building or comprehension-causing activity just because it went from paper to computer screen. Clicking with a mouse on the right or wrong answer or filling in the right or wrong answer with a pencil are similarly limited and superficial. The computer may be fun versus the paper and pencil, but each approach functions at the level of worksheet superficiality. There is no real reason to expect that students can be worksheeted into wisdom, textbooked into brilliance, videoed into academic achievement, or Friday-tested into making an extraordinary commitment to school, to learning, and to thinking.

What is to be done? Perhaps a significant systemic reform of education could help. The federal government, state governments, local governments, school boards, and school district central offices could revise their laws, policies, and organization charts. Can an efficient, service-driven, customer friendly bureaucracy ensure that Tasha can read and Shawn can write? Some changes in organizational structure, laws, policies, and management methods are better than others, but Tasha's reading and Shawn's writing are not directly impacted by new, improved bureaucracies. Improvements in bureaucratic structure or operations may be well-intentioned and honorable, but their impact on students is limited and indirect. Students who read well or poorly are not reading well or poorly because the bureaucracy moved Reading Support Services from one office to another. The new, improved bureaucracy may be as much of an illusion as putting the paper worksheet onto a computer screen.

So, what is to be done? There are no secrets, no surprises, and no simple solutions. The good news is that students can achieve great academic results. We know what causes great academic results. These results do not come easily, but they are possible. In classrooms throughout the United States, great teaching is causing great learning daily. What is being done in these classrooms?

According to research I have done during the past ten years, research my graduate school students have done during the past five years, and teaching experiences I have had with middle school and high school students for twenty-one years, here is what happens in the classrooms of great academic achievement:

1. Teachers challenge students.
2. Teachers are enthusiastic about teaching, learning, and students.
3. Teachers use a variety of teaching methods and activities.
4. Teachers connect learning with students' real lives.

I have asked some three thousand people questions about great teachers. The answers always are consistent with the four general conclusions listed above. Graduate school students of mine have asked similar questions to about five hundred more people. Those answers provide additional confirmation. We know what great teachers do in their classrooms and how they teach. The teaching activities and teaching methods of great teachers are available for everyone to use. It is likely that great teachers expect themselves to do great work and find much benefit from their work. Great teachers do not always realize their greatness; rather, they would accept nothing less and simply see their great teaching as a personal duty and as a personal standard. They are more demanding of themselves than any personnel evaluation could be.

There's more that relates to how a teacher views teaching and views the job description of teacher, if that job description exists. Is teaching a job through which a teacher provides an opportunity for each student to learn by presenting an activity that each student is expected to do? Is teaching a job in which the teacher teaches and the students follow along with what he or she presents?

Try this: a teacher's job is to cause learning by each student and by the teacher. With that understanding of a teacher's job, different work will be done by a teacher and by students than if the teaching job is seen as giving students a series of worksheets to complete, textbook chapters to read, videos to watch, and generic tests to take on Friday. My most recent book, *Extreme Learning*, showed the magnificent impact on one teacher and on her teaching when she realized that the job of teacher is searching for and experiencing dynamic interaction that causes learning. When she saw herself as a person whose job is to cause learning—not as a person who serves as a classroom clerk annually repeating 175 days of pointless, meaningless, superficial, prepackaged academic baby food—she came alive in the classroom and her students became energized.

In the past few years I have explored what great students do to become successful at school. My interest grew when I taught an eighth grade economics class of students with prior grade point averages ranging from 1.5 to 4.0; however, in this economics class almost all students earned an A. Another economics class had students with a grade point average range of 2.0 to 3.1; however, twenty-one students in the class earned an A and two students earned a B. What characteristics, work habits, personal traits, and other ingredients produce great students? How can greatness be inspired in students and nurtured, applied, encouraged, challenged, and developed in students? What classroom activities and atmosphere can best inspire and nurture great students?

Since writing and rereading *Extreme Teaching* and *Extreme Learning*, I realize that I am best as a teacher when I am most extreme in my teaching—making connections between the wholesome knowledge, interests, and talents of students and what they need to learn. I expect myself to learn as much as the students learn. I will learn about the students, individually and as a classroom group, and I will learn about how these students learn, individually and as a classroom group. These extreme insights guide the instructional design work I do to create classroom activities, experiences, interactions, and challenges that will cause each and every student to learn. I constantly revise my teaching method because no two groups of students are alike; no two students are alike and no one student is the same every day.

This might suggest to some people that extreme teachers who cause extreme learning with and for extreme students have to do endless amounts of extra work. I love to teach and I love to learn, so the work I do to prepare for classes is very enjoyable. My job duty is to cause learning. That result is not obtained through seven or eight hours per day. I do not work endlessly, but I know that sufficient time invested is one essential element of greatness in any endeavor. While a classroom clerk spends an hour at the copy machine duplicating ordinary publisher-prepared worksheets that were created by someone who does not know the classroom clerk's students, I invest an hour creating fascinating classroom activities that will cause learning. The worksheets will get a bell-shaped curve or worse result. The activities I create will inspire, motivate, and teach everyone in the class. What prepackaged worksheets may seem to offer in efficiency is lost in the minimal results they get. "You guys have to keep doing this worksheet until you get it right" is an indictment of the worksheet method, not the students. Extreme teachers who cause extreme learning rarely have to reteach because the students actually learned the ideas the first time.

Just as the methods of great teachers are available to all teachers, the methods used by great students can be made available to all students, with two disclaimers: (1) students who are criminals, are approaching criminal status, or are incorrigible need to be educated in hybrid jails/schools or in highly structured alternative programs because their issues go beyond what can be resolved by a change of teaching method in a regular classroom, and (2) students with severe mental health or mental functioning conditions need unique educational approaches provided by talented educators and other providers to maximize their achievement.

What is an extreme student? He or she is a student in elementary school, middle school, or high school who has an eager, lively, wholesome intellectual curiosity that drives him or her to academic greatness class after class, day after day, year after year.

How are extreme students created, inspired, nurtured, encouraged, and taught? What classroom atmosphere, environment, teaching methods, and learning activities help maximize the academic achievement of extreme students? What classroom activities and atmosphere can propel a student from his or her current apathetic attitude about school into the extreme student attitude? What classroom activities and atmosphere can inspire the "I just want to get by" student into the extreme student commitment to infinite learning? The purpose of this book is to answer those questions while adding some bonus insights, wisdom, ideas, encouragement, and inspiration.

Several years ago when I interviewed for a high school principal position, the final question posed to the eight of us in the awkward group interview screening process was, "If we visited the campus of your high school when you are principal, what would we see?" I knew my answer immediately.

The first response from another candidate was "the campus and the building would be very clean." I spoke next with a neutral tone, a confident smile, and a direct contrast with the first answer. "You would see ideas. Students and teachers would be encountering ideas, creating ideas, exploring ideas, challenging ideas, and mutually learning as they pushed the frontier of ideas." I did not get past the screening interview. The person who spoke of a clean campus was selected for the job. No doubt, a clean campus is desirable. A campus of ideas is essential. We can have both, but ideas are more important.

If your top priority is a clean campus or a clean classroom, read another book. If your top priority is the meaningful and fascinating adventure of learning, then please read, encounter, interact with, and challenge the ideas in this book.

Keen J. Babbage
March 2005

Chapter 1

Please Break Some Old Habits

"Open your books to page 63. Chapter 3 starts on that page. Take the next fifteen minutes to read section 1 of chapter 3 and write answers to the think and remember questions at the end of section 1. Do not go past section 1. I'll collect your papers in fifteen minutes and then we can watch the video that goes along with chapter 3. We may have time at the end of class to look at the overhead projector pictures that go with chapter 3, section 1. If there are no questions, begin reading now."

I have a question. What evidence suggests that chapter 3, section 1, and the accompanying video plus matching overhead slides is the best way to teach Tasha and Shawn?

Tasha hears the generic assignment and knows that she will easily and effortlessly complete it in less than fifteen minutes. She thinks to herself, "This is so boring. I hope I stay awake! The last time I fell asleep in this class I got in trouble. The book is so dull. The video will be so stupid. The slides we'll look at are dumb. This class is so boring."

Shawn is in the same class. He thinks to himself, "No problem. This is so easy. Who needs to read anything. The questions are nothing. I can answer them in no time just by finding a few words in the chapter. Easy A. Same thing every day. This class is so easy."

Tasha and Shawn can do much more than read a few textbook pages and answer a few ordinary questions that require no thinking and are not worth remembering despite the bold print and fancy font heading of "Think and Remember" atop the generic questions. The teacher is in the habit of reading textbook pages, answering textbook questions, watching a video, observing overhead slides, collecting papers, bell ringing, students leaving, other students entering, repeating process. This sequence does very little for the students or the teacher. So much more can be done if the teacher breaks the predictable habit and boldly explores ideas, learning activities, knowledge, discussions, interaction, questions, re-search, writing, drawing, inventing, discovery, and learning with the students. "Please break some old habits" is the unspoken hope of Tasha for this teacher. Shawn likes the easy A that comes with playing school, but his grade would mean something if dynamic teaching and learning experiences were provided. The teacher would also benefit from breaking some of the old habits. The textbook –questions–video–overhead sequence does not enable the teacher to know students, learn how students learn, vibrantly interact with students, or design effective teaching activities that fill the classroom with learning as a partnership between a teacher and students who learn with, from, and about each other.

Textbooks, textbook questions, videos, and overhead slides—all part of prepackaged, finite, limited instructional materials that are commonly available and commonly used—are to teaching and learning what plain white bread is to nutrition. Healthy, nutritious meals include a variety of foods rather than slice after slice of white bread.

I have asked thousands of people to tell me about the best teacher they remember, the best teaching they experienced, the most significant learning they experienced. No person has ever mentioned a textbook, questions at the end of a textbook chapter section, worksheets, videos, or overhead projector. Responses to my questions always emphasize people—what they did to cause learning, what they did to inspire thinking, how they motivated students through personal expressions of concern, confidence, and challenge.

Textbooks, textbook questions, worksheets, videos, and overhead projector slides could be used as a small part of the teaching and learning experiences in a highly productive classroom, but they should not be the habitual and only tasks done daily in a classroom where the routine rules, the teacher watches, the students endure, and after Friday's test most of what was "learned" is forgotten because it served no purpose, had no meaning, and made no connection except a grade on Friday's superficial, simplistic test.

Extreme students are not created, inspired, or nurtured by ordinary, predictable, generic, impersonal, limited, and schoolish instructional habits, routines, and procedures. Schoolish means serving a purpose restricted to a school-imposed obligation or routine such as Friday's test but having little or no value, application, or connection with any other part of life.

Extreme students have a relentless curiosity, a determined drive to know more, a thirst for knowledge, a hunger for wisdom, an urge to discover why, a commitment to learning, and a high personal standard for how learning is pursued. Extreme students master all the basic requirements of a curriculum and then search for a deeper, wider, longer degree of knowledge, understanding, application, and mastery. Extreme students are created, inspired, nurtured, and challenged by extreme teachers who cause extreme learning.

Extreme students are created, inspired, nurtured, and challenged when classroom experiences connect with the wholesome knowledge, talents, and interests of students; when learning is real right now; when a teacher is enthusiastic; when a variety of teaching methods are used; when no two classroom days are exactly alike; when student ideas, suggestions, and input help shape classroom activities; when connections are made; when choices are given; and when interaction is personal, lively, and genuine.

Why are extreme students desirable? Educators have an ethical obligation to provide experiences that enable students to maximize their abilities, which is another way of saying to become extreme students. Colleges, universities, and employers increasingly seek students or graduates who are able to think critically, solve problems, work with a team, innovate, communicate effectively, and take initiative. Those characteristics are inherent within the process of extreme teaching causing extreme learning as extreme students are created, inspired, nurtured, and challenged.

Teachers can learn from and with extreme students. Teachers learn little or nothing from or with students who sit and complete worksheets. Teachers benefit from creating and inspiring extreme students. Teaching extreme students is a vastly different career experience than teaching textbookers and worksheeters whose only goal is to get out of class as soon as possible. But what if extreme students get out of control and disrupt class? When students are fascinated by the learning activities in the classroom, they commit themselves to cooperating with the teacher and one another. Fascinated students are academically lively, yet they behave well. Bored, frustrated, "can't take another worksheet," "can't watch another video" students are much more likely to misbehave at school than are extreme students.

When teachers break the routine habits associated with ordinary, mundane classroom tasks and provide real, meaningful, fascinating classroom adventures, students are less likely to violate school rules.

Schools today are asked to, told to, required to accomplish more than ever before. Each student is to master the fundamentals of the curriculum and all students are to demonstrate proficiency across a range of skills, knowledge, and subjects. Those ambitious and challenging goals can be reached with ambitious and challenging teaching methods that cause extreme learning as they inspire extreme students.

When teachers attend "professional development" programs, what are their most common complaints? These are the two complaints I have heard from teachers whom I asked to evaluate most programs, workshops, conferences or presentations they have attended: (1) it was boring, (2) none of it applies to me or to what I do.

Are teachers fully attentive at professional development programs? Do teachers stay "on-task" 100 percent of the time at professional development programs? Do teachers model perfect student behavior when attending professional development programs? I have heard many educators say, "If our students behaved in class the way we behave in our professional development programs, the students would get in trouble."

One reason teachers sometimes are not fully attentive, fully on-task, and completely well-behaved at professional development sessions is that the presentation is a lecture punctuated with handouts, overhead projector slides, and an occasional question answered with generalizations. The audience is not involved, the material is not practical, the only anticipation is for lunch, and the only hope is that the afternoon session will conclude ahead of schedule. When teachers acknowledge their negative reaction to professional development programs they are, perhaps without realizing, identifying reasons why so many students have a negative attitude toward and a limited commitment to school. Even students with positive attitudes and solid commitments could have better experiences if all of their classes were as good as their best class.

Teachers would like for the habits of typical professional development training programs to be broken. Teachers would like the training sessions to be fascinating, useful, real, connected to their job, and done in ways that exemplify superior teaching. Students cannot be textbooked and worksheeted into mastery, proficiency, brilliance, and commitment. Teachers cannot be professionally developed via a prepackaged, generic lecture especially when the lecturer is not a person who does or could do the demanding job the teacher will return to the classroom to do. Teachers would prefer that their training programs be done in an extreme teaching way so extreme learning is caused and the teacher as a student of teaching becomes an extreme student. The habits of some professional development programs need to be broken too. The need is real and urgent, so why wait?

Educators can separate themselves, their students, and their schools from the ordinary, the superficial, the routine, the average, the limited, the prepackaged, the generic, the rerun, and the plain. Educators can do for their classrooms and their students what the stars do for, to, and with anyone who looks deeply into the clear night sky—remind us of the adventurous beyond, the unlimited frontier, the depth of what can be known when thought and attention penetrate profoundly through the obvious or the superficial, and the inspirational power of searching for what can be known. Education can be as deep as the soul and as vast as the universe, as unlimited as thought itself and as personal as your name. There are no inherent limits to what education can be and can include. If limits have been imposed on educational experiences, they can be removed.

There are many difficulties facing schools today. From the federal government increasing its interference in education to state and local governments confronting limited budgets, from insufficient alternative education options to ineffective juvenile justice programs, from apathetic students to confrontational parents and guardians, from belligerent community groups blaming school for all of society's ills to advocacy groups whose members have never worked in schools telling people who do work in schools how to do their jobs, the list of difficulties facing schools is long. Despite that reality and the frustrations it can cause, there is hope. Of all the variables that impact education, educators control the most important one—the effectiveness of what is done in classrooms. There is a personal, professional, and ethical peace given to every teacher who provides the very best classroom experience for his or her students.

Despite all of the difficulties that the federal government, the local newspaper, the radio talk-show guest, the loud citizens group, the belligerent parent or guardian, the court-involved student or the just-waiting-for-retirement teacher creates for schools, there is still a wonderful freedom and a potent power available to teachers—to create and to provide absolutely fascinating classroom activities that cause learning. "But Keen, you don't know my students or my school." True, I have not met your young scholars or visited your school. I have worked in four different schools. I have been the assistant principal and a teacher at an urban middle school for twelve years. I work face-to-face every day with students by choice. Where are the important education battles won and where are the essential education results obtained? In classrooms in schools and that is where I work, so you and I have much in common. Although the specifics of our workplaces differ, the nature of the challenges is similar and we can reason together to share ideas, trade success stories, invent solutions, and encourage each other.

Please break the habit of seeing teaching as a process through which all students, class after class, year after year, are given a finite, repetitious sequence of classroom tasks limited to use of textbooks, worksheets, videos, and generic publisher-provided tests. Knowledge does not fit into a textbook. Creative ideas and critical thinking are not developed by worksheets. Watching video after video is similar to watching hour after hour of television—passive and unproductive. Prepackaged materials that come with textbooks may appear to provide abundant supplemental resources such as worksheets, a quiz to go with each chapter, a test to use with each chapter, but these materials are not designed for the students in your classroom. These generic materials are designed for generic students who, if given a steady week after week process of these materials will get nothing more than a generic, fill-in-the-blank, wordsearch, solve-the-puzzle, complete-the-riddle, and answer-the-question-in-the space-provided education. That process of education relies on printing presses and copy machines. Real, meaningful, useful, profound education relies on brain-to-brain, face-to-face, idea-to-idea, question-to-answer interaction between a teacher and students. Please, if you are in the habit of "Today is Monday, start reading section 1 of chapter 11, just as we always read section 1 of a new chapter on Monday . . ." break that habit. Even if you use amazingly creative classroom activities, resist the idea of taking your favorite lessons from recent years and combining those into a year of reruns. What was a creative, effective lesson last year with last year's students may not work today with today's students, who bring a unique collection of individual and group knowledge, interests and talents.

"But Keen, you must think that my students are really smart and can do all kinds of different work. At least they go along with the textbook routine."

The extreme students category is not limited to honor roll students, gifted and talented students, perfectly behaved students, high IQ students, or "most likely to succeed" students. Those students may be doing well in school, but are they being given the maximum academic challenge and are they experiencing learning in ways that stretch them beyond a "this is easy" comfort zone into a "this is hard but fascinating" extreme student zone.

Students who are doing average work, below average work, or are failing could become extreme students. Those students bring wholesome knowledge, interests, and talents with them to school, but what they are expected to learn at school and how they are required to learn it never connect with what they have made wholesome commitments to and are willing to make new commitments to. For those students, school is to be endured and life is to be lived, but the two do not overlap.

Extreme students have a wholesome, energetic, determined intellectual curiosity for knowledge. They probably have interests beyond academics—soccer, becoming an Eagle Scout, marching band, volunteer work in the community, family responsibilities, part-time jobs, church youth group, summer camps, and more—and in those activities they are also intellectually eager for knowledge, depth of understanding, success, significance, challenge, and direction to know how and where to find the next new challenge or adventure that will emerge from encountering and mastering the most recent challenge and adventure.

Elementary school, middle school, and high school students are inclined toward the extreme. Some trends, fads, innovations, and opportunities begin with the student age group. Yes, adults sometimes have to guide the direction of those trends to keep students within the boundaries of safety, law, morality, and wholesomeness, but youthful eagerness for that which is new, neat, innovative, cool, awesome, and extreme is eagerness that can be applied in classrooms at school. There is an extreme student potential in each young scholar in each classroom. When given extreme learning experiences, the extreme student will emerge, learn, and succeed.

Please break some of the habits of teaching by prepackaged formulas. Require that students break their habits of playing school by passively accepting prepackaged, superficial work on their part as the best work they can do or should try.

Please break some of the rules also, including those you impose on yourself through inertia, routine, "it's the way we've always done it," or other rationalizations. Textbooks can be used productively in classrooms as one of many resources, but textbooks should not rule the classroom or the curriculum.

Please break some of the habits and rules. That's right. Please break, destroy, obliterate, and abandon some of the habits and rules. Please rise above the routine of the rules. Please liberate yourself and your students from the limitations of the habits and the rules. You can and must remain ethical, moral, legal, and professional as you boldly journey beyond the habits and the rules, but there is much unchartered, frontier academic territory beyond the habits and the rules that is still within the guidelines of ethics, morality, law, and professional standards. Imagine what could be achieved if the only habit were to have no restrictive, unproductive habits and the only rule were to have no restrictive, unproductive rules.

One great sadness about schools and classrooms may be that rules rule. Create a classroom where thinking rules, where creativity rules, where imagination rules, where learning rules, where potent questions rule, where spontaneous innovation rules, where the rule is to rise above all rules.

Break the habits and the rules of textbooks, worksheets, tests on Friday, and the tyranny of the time-release justification of education that is expressed in "you'll need to know this later in life for middle school, high school, or college." Textbooks are limited to the superficial summaries that fit into thirty-two chapters, each divided into sections ending with mundane, ordinary, predictable, empty, mirror-image of the text questions. Section 1 on Monday, section 2 on Tuesday, section 3 on Wednesday, section 4 and a quiz on Thursday, test on Friday followed by "sit quietly until everyone is finished and then you may talk until the bell rings," real life on Saturday and Sunday, followed by section 1 of the next chapter on Monday. That sequence will not advance students to meaningful mastery, productive proficiency, or a commitment to significant success at school. That sequence will not provide teachers with meaningful career experiences or significant interaction with students. There are few if any real winners, when mundane habits, unproductive rules, and ordinary routines prevail.

Break the habit and the rule of video, DVD, CD, or other formats that are similar in impact. "Watch this video for forty-two minutes. You'll have a quiz on this tomorrow if I can find the quiz that came with the video. Plus, this video has some information you'll need when you get to college." Extreme teachers occasionally use videos, but they preview the video and use only the essential, effective two minutes of it to enhance learning during a multiactivity class period that includes thinking, writing, interacting, discussing, drawing, questioning, and two cleverly timed one-minute video clips.

Break the habits and the rules. Of course, schools need rules about walking in the halls, being on time for class, and much more to maintain a safe, healthy, orderly atmosphere. Keep those rules, in fact get very serious about safety, security, and proper behavior. Use surveillance cameras, metal detectors, and school law enforcement officers. Safety and security methods at schools need frequent updating just as instructional methods do.

Break, outsmart, improve, liberate from, go beyond the mental habits and rules, the learning habits and rules, the routine habits and rules that make school a routine rather than an extreme adventure, break the habit and rule of school is boring, break the habit and rule of "when you are in college" as the answer to "when will we ever use this in real life." Be extreme.

Let's personalize the idea of breaking habits and breaking rules with two real-life stories. A sixth grader walked up to me as he went through the cafeteria serving line that I supervise for two hours daily. He smiled and said, "You're a great teacher." I thanked him for the very kind and gracious comment. What was the basis for his conclusion? Earlier on that day I taught his math class. I offer that service to teachers so they can observe their colleagues teach and so they can observe how students learn in another class. I had been told that the students needed to do some worksheet practice and review about fractions. The teacher agreed that I would create a lesson dealing with fractions that used different materials and methods.

Class began with this comment, "Hi. I'm Dr. Babbage. I get to be your math teacher today. I know some of you, but let's take a minute for every one to take a turn and tell me your first name." With that completed, each student and I had made direct, eye-to-eye, person-to-person contact. I then said, "We need to admit something about fractions that math books never tell you and math teachers usually do not tell you, but it is true and everyone knows it. Here goes. Raise your hand, please, if you think fractions are weird." Every student immediately, energetically, and with absolute conviction raised a hand. "You are right. We agree on that and we admit that. It's okay to say that fractions are weird. We are in total agreement. Now, put your hands down and let's make sense out of weird fractions." We then used sports statistics, drawings, pictures, money, and their input to make sense out of fractions.

As I moved through the room it was obvious that one student was not paying attention to math, but he was completely absorbed in his work to break his pencil into several pieces. He did not expect to become our most effective practical application of fractions. "This is perfect. Here we have what used to one whole pencil, but now it is in four fairly equal parts. What could we call each of these parts? I'll count to three and everyone answer. One, two, three . . ." There was a wonderful chorus of thirty-one sixth graders proudly proclaiming "one-fourth." The student who had been playing with his pencil shouted "one-fourth" eagerly and paid perfect attention during the rest of class. At lunch he said to me, "You're a great teacher." I asked him what he remembered about class. "Well, I was tearing up my pencil and you said I was making it into fractions. That was neat." I asked him if he saw any fractions in the lunch serving line. "Yeah, that orange has been cut into pieces and so has the pizza." He had learned about fractions, he had learned something about learning, he had discovered an unexpected connection between his curiosity and fractions. He was ready, willing, and able to think more about fractions. He had discovered an intellectual curiosity within. He can become an extreme student who has extreme success at school.

The discussion of parents, guardians, teachers, and school administrators was about how to most effectively allocate school funds for classroom instructional materials. One comment startled me when I concluded that the speaker did not realize the wisdom and the truth she was so close to reaching. "I keep hoping that I can get the students to want to learn something because then they will get to do something cool with it."

The reader knows what the next sentence will be, so please join me: "If you did something cool with it, the students would want to learn it." Doing something cool does not mean doing something easy, amusing, entertaining, or useless. Doing something cool means participating in classroom learning activities that fascinate, intrigue, surprise, inform, amaze, connect; are interactive, meaningful, challenging; and inspire an eager, wholesome curiosity to know more, know better, know fully. These extreme learning results can be obtained through extreme teaching methods; however, great results will not come from ordinary teaching methods.

One of American's nineteeth-century writers of conscience and intellect, Henry David Thoreau, concluded that "the surface of the earth is soft and impressible by the feet of men; and so with the paths which the mind travels. How worn and dusty, then, must be the highways of the world, how deep the cuts of tradition and conformity! I did not wish to take a cabin passage, but rather to go before the mast and on the deck of the world, for there I could best see the moonlight amid the mountains. I do not wish to go below now."[1]

Thoreau sought extreme learning to satisfy his wholesome intellectual curiosities. He was an extreme student who perfected idiosyncrasies that some people would choose not to follow. However, he continues to impact thinkers and readers despite having written two centuries ago. Extreme students can be found throughout history and can be inspired in classrooms today. Thoreau's concern and caution about conformity and tradition that etch ruts into the mind is similar to my concern about conformity to traditional teaching methods that fill the minutes of a class but not the mind of a student.

Middle school and high school students bring minds, personalities, ideas, experiences, questions, curiosities, knowledge, talents, and interests to school with them. Their brains are ready and eager for more than a task or an assignment; rather, their brains thrive on an adventurous, creative, interactive, fascinating challenge. Even if this challenge seems overwhelming, the brain will make new connections, create new synaptic actions, and organize its wiring to master the new intellectual endeavor. Ordinary teaching methods are brainly boring. Teach so classes are brainfully fascinating. Extreme students need to experience brainfully extreme learning activities. The brains of our students can do much more than they are commonly required to do. The brain will eagerly respond to a fascinating challenge.

Another habit and rule to break is a common cliché: "We must teach our children well because they are our future." Students are also part of the right here, right now, present. Students deserve the most effective, meaningful, useful, and fascinating educational experience now because students are real people who are living real lives right now. When education becomes personal, interpersonal, and real, then it matters now and students fully commit to education.

I do use "thinksheets" in my classes. These are materials that I design for the students and are based on two factors: (1) what the students need to learn and (2) what wholesome knowledge, interests, and talents I have discovered that those students bring with them to class or have developed during class. The thinksheet causes learning by making connections between what the students need to learn and what they already know. No third party supplier of instructional materials

knows my students personally, so to make learning personal and interpersonal—
which means to make it real and worth working to obtain, I design the materials
we use in class. Thinksheets can help cause whatever learning goal I have set for
the class today. Generic "store bought" worksheets cannot compete with my
homemade, personal, fascinating, creative thinksheets. Even extreme teachers
use the copier, but we do not live at it and we do not make copies of anything prefabricated, prepackaged, generic, ordinary, or impersonal.

One habit or rule that endures is the "we have so much to cover" perspective.
Covering material does not equal knowing the subject, mastering the concept, or
applying the skills. "Covering material" means "we went over adding fractions
last week. Don't you remember that?" Students do not achieve academic proficiency merely by spending time in a classroom where curriculum-related material is "covered" or textbook pages and worksheets are "gone over."

Learning via exploring ideas, rather than covering or going over multiple bits
of information, facts, or dates, can be more fascinating. Reflecting on the idea of
a fraction—"It's like that slice of a pizza, you know, it's a part of the pizza" or
"Well, the First Amendment says I have freedom of speech, so why can't I speak
at a high school assembly and tell the other students what I think after the guest
speaker talks" can be much more effective, productive, and fascinating than
merely crunching the numbers of problems 1 to 21 on page 57 in the math book
or reading section 1 of chapter 6 in the United States government book. Yes, some
math problems need to be worked, step by step, by hand. Yes, some written content in social studies needs to be read. Beginning with and becoming intrigued
with the idea of a fraction or the idea of a constitutional right creates a reason to
do the math or do the reading.

When students think about math ideas and then eagerly do math problems with
the driving power of curiosity inspired by the big idea, they can truly know math.
When students pedantically do math problem after math problem just to cover the
math material or merely go over the math material the students may know about
math, but they are less likely to know math. Knowing math includes seeing how
math connects with life, seeing how math is used right now in purposeful ways,
solving the puzzle that math can be, doing math for its compelling sense of satisfaction that comes with genuine mental struggle resulting in eventual mental success. Students who master math and are proficient in math know math rather than
just know about math.

Some classroom habits include the "it's Wednesday so we will work in groups
today" or the "everyone always does his or her own individual work. No working in groups." Group work should be used when it is the best way to cause the
intended learning, not because it has been one week since we last did group work.
Learning can expand when two or more brains team up to complete a well-
designed, well-supervised learning activity. The individual brain can learn without limit. Two brains interacting can learn with a depth, an efficiency, and a sym-
biosis that is confirmed whenever one participant in the group says, "Wow, I

never thought of that" in response to another student's idea, explanation, insight, question, conclusion, or terminology.

If the wording of this chapter's challenge—break some of the old habits and break some of the old rules—seems harsh, bothersome, or drastic, change the wording and begin with smaller steps such as revise the rules, adjust the habits, but keep revising and keep adjusting until better results are obtained. Get out of the "we've always done it this way" rule or the "I've always done it that way" habit. The goal is to cause learning, not perpetuate the implementation of rules and habits that provide adequate results or unacceptable results.

The current results in education often are evaluated as below the acceptable level. Successful students need new challenges. Average or unsuccessful students need to reach mastery and proficiency levels. The same evaluation is true for businesses seeking to compete successfully—they must constantly improve, innovate, evaluate, and update. A democratic, capitalistic society always expects improvements in production, product quality, innovation, and results.

Most cars coming off modern assembly lines are well made, but recalls to correct manufacturing errors still happen. It is probably easier to control the manufacturing process of a car than the educational process of a student—the car cannot resist being assembled and the car cannot lose its homework. But even with that superior control, errors happen. Car companies do seek to minimize errors and maximize quality performance. The automobile design, production, and distribution process is updated often. No car company does business as it did forty years ago, twenty years ago, or ten years ago. Successful manufacturers break old habits and break old rules to take advantage of new ideas and remain current in today's marketplace. The marketplace changes and successful companies must keep up or, better yet, set the pace.

The educational marketplace is the classroom. Students of each generation are different. Students within each generation are different. Each classroom group of students brings collective uniqueness and individually unique knowledge, interests, and talents. The extreme teacher builds on, applies, seeks to know each group's personality and uniqueness while also learning about each individual's knowledge, interests, and talents because these insights identify and serve as vital teaching resources. Extreme teachers who cause extreme learning for and with extreme students are not textbookers, worksheeters, or video players. They are teachers. They cause learning. They design, engineer, and produce learning with insight, care, and concern that surpasses the precision of any sophisticated manufacturing process because the human adventures of thinking and of learning have no assembly line limits. Extreme teaching is hard work, but causing extreme learning and inspiring extreme students is an ultimate reward. Teachers thrive on that reward for work which exhausts the body yet nourishes and renews the heart, mind, and soul.

Breaking some of the old habits and old rules of education, school, classrooms, teaching is intended to release the dynamic potential of students and teachers to think without unnecessary limits, learn without unnecessary restrictions, and commit to active membership in a learning community without reservation.

What students learn at school is important and can be a significant factor in creating, inspiring, nurturing, and challenging extreme students. How students learn at school—the moment-to-moment, class-to-class, subject-to-subject, day-to-day classroom experiences that are designed to cause learning—is an equally (if not more) important factor in the development of extreme students. What is to be taught is usually decided for teachers by school councils, school boards, or state government authorities. How teaching is done remains an area in education where teachers often have much freedom, many options, and abundant control. The teacher's career is enhanced and the students' learning is enhanced when only the most effective teaching methods are used. Revise or eliminate all teaching methods that do not maximize student achievement. Such revising and eliminating are easier said than done but are possible, necessary, and ethically mandatory.

I have noticed through many years of evaluating and analyzing grade point averages at several schools that most students who make the honor roll for their superior grades are on the honor roll report card after report card. Conversely, most students who do not make the honor roll consistently are off the honor roll with a steady C average or lower. I have also noticed that some honor roll students do not work very hard on their classes but know how to do enough to earn a B average or better. There are some students who have a very wholesome intellectual curiosity for knowledge and they often make good grades, but they seek to know more than what some good grades measure. It intrigues me that "wholesome intellectual curiosity for knowledge" becomes the acronym WICK, the part of a candle or lamp that absorbs fuel, burns, and helps illuminate. That is similar to what a wholesome intellectual curiosity for knowledge does for the brain, the mind, and the extreme student—it absorbs the fuel of ideas and learning, it burns with a dedication to find answers and insights; it illuminates itself and colleagues with understanding and discovery. Extreme students have a wholesome intellectual curiosity for knowledge. Their curiosity is more satisfied through learning experiences that emerge when some of the old habits and some of the old rules are broken.

How do I know this is true? The research that will be presented in chapter 4 offers support. My daily experience with students offers further support. From October though December 2004 I taught eighth grade economics to students who brought extreme student tendencies with them and became exemplary extreme students. What did they learn and how did they learn it? I asked them that question often, and their answers further convince me to keep breaking some of the old habits and some of the old rules because today's students deserve original opportunities to think and learn in the most productive ways; those ways are unique to every class and to each student because each student is a unique being.

I told the young scholars in economics class at the beginning of our first class together that "I know that you will master the seventeen economic vocabulary terms that are the core content requirements for eighth graders in economics. I know what we will do in class today and tomorrow. Beyond that, what you learn and how you learn it will be created as I learn about you, about your wholesome knowledge, talents, and interests, about how you learn individually and about how you learn together." Their learning surpassed every goal I set and every dream I envisioned. They became very extreme students. They learned much, they were excited about class, they became learning partners with me and with one another, they sought depths of knowledge, and they said they were sorry to see the class end. The pursuit and achievement of that type of experience with students confirms to me that some of the old habits and some of the old rules must be broken.

For college students or graduate school students who have not begun your teaching career yet, you do not have old habits to break and old rules to break, or do you? You are in habits as a student. You and your teachers have used rules and routines. Do not teach the way your teachers taught you. Use some of the best teaching methods, activities, ideas, beliefs, attitudes, and convictions of your best teachers. Use your own best ideas. Still, expect to innovate, create, and build as you learn about your students and as you realize how your students learn.

The purpose of a school is to cause learning. The measure of teaching is that students at school learned the curriculum of the school and went as much further than and deeper than the curriculum as possible. The resulting definition of a teacher is a person who causes proper, intended learning. For all of that to happen schools and teachers need to use the most effective teaching methods and activities possible, consistent with law, policy, and professional ethical standards. Of course, laws and policies can be changed if they are outdated, unproductive, or are in the category of habits and rules that need to be broken. Breaking the textbook habit or the rule of worksheets does not violate a law, policy, or professional ethical standard. The intention of the ideas in this chapter is to encourage classroom learning activities that get results for teachers and students, not to begin revolutionary acts of defiance or civil disobedience that disrupt education or end careers. If a law, policy, or regulation limits effective teaching and wholesome learning, work relentlessly to change that law, policy, or regulation, but do not blatantly defy it because that is unprofessional and unethical. Defy the textbook habit and defy the rule of worksheets—those actions are honorable.

We move now from the philosophical and attitudinal foundation established in this chapter to a series of personal testimonials of what can be accomplished when extreme teachers cause extreme learning by and with extreme students. We will contrast those results with what happens when classroom experiences are plain, ordinary, generic, and superficial.

NOTE

1. Henry David Thoreau, *Walden*, Bantam Classic ed. (New York: Bantam, 1981), 343.

Chapter 2

What Can Be; What Might Have Been

Dear School Board Members,
Thank you for your recent letter. I appreciate your friendly words of congratula-
tions about my recent graduation from high school. I think it is really cool that
you would write to all of the graduates. I am really impressed that you are ask-
ing my opinion of the schools I attended in this town. Here's what I think. I'm
pretty direct and blunt, but you asked for the truth and I'm glad to be honest with
you. Hey, I'm already a graduate so nothing can happen to me, right? It's too late
to send me to the principal's office.

I have some memories of elementary school, but it's been a long time so there's
not much to say. I liked elementary school and I think everyone liked it. Teachers
were friendly. We got to do a lot of different activities in classes. We had lots of work
to do, but music, skits, concerts, plays, art projects, recess, and holiday celebrations
made everything seem really enjoyable. We did extra work on reading. Some days it
seemed like we did nothing but read. Our teachers were obsessed with reading.

It took me a few weeks to adjust to middle school, but my friends and I figured
it out by September of our sixth grade year. Read the chapter. Answer the ques-
tions. Do the homework, do the worksheets. Cram answers into my head the night
before or the minute before a test. Don't pass social notes in class. Get to class
on time. Keep your hands to yourself when teachers are watching. Always have a
pencil and some paper. Stay out of trouble. Middle school was easy. I made good
grades, but I really don't remember much of the stuff I studied.

There was one middle school teacher who was cool. She was like an actress in
class and we never knew what the next event in class might be. I remember she
had us read the entire Declaration of Independence word for word. The book just
had a sentence or two of the Declaration of Independence, but she insisted that
educated, civilized people must know everything about the important events and
ideas from history.

She had people from the school and from our city, even radio and television announcers, tape record the Declaration of Independence. We really paid attention when she played that tape because we wondered whose voice we might hear next. It was so cool when my favorite radio announcer read a few sentences. And when the famous football coach from a nearby university read a sentence we went crazy. I still remember that. Of course, the teacher made us do tons of work about the Declaration of Independence, but that tape was so cool that doing the other work did not really seem like work. I remember doing research on Thomas Jefferson. I had to present it in class as an interview with Jefferson so I got that radio announcer to come to class and read Jefferson's answers. That was so cool. Most of the rest of middle school was the typical stuff with books and tests.

High school was great. There was so much to do. I'm sure we were supposed to work a lot harder and learn a lot more. Get real. Most classes were pretty much alike with longer, thicker textbooks to read and more questions to answer. It just seemed like middle school had expanded. But there were so many other cool things to do. I played soccer. We did work hard in soccer and we did learn a lot about soccer. My soccer coach taught one class I had in my junior year. He made us work a lot harder in soccer than in class, but nobody complained.

Some of the high school teachers were pretty different. My physics teacher could be an astronaut, he knows so much about science. His classroom was like one of those children museum places where everything is science, but you actually walk into the experiment and become part of the experiment.

My high school theater and drama teacher used television soap operas to get us interested. Then we created our own high school soap opera. We even listened to some old radio program soap operas from the 1930s. That class was cool.

So, you want my advice about school? Go visit my high school physics teacher, my high school theater teacher, and my middle school U.S. history teacher. Get other teachers to do what they do.

Sincerely,
Julie Johnson

⁜

Dear School Board Members,
Thanks for attending our high school graduation event and thanks for the letter congratulating each graduate. I guess you were serious when you asked us to tell you our opinions about school. First, I never write letters. I don't know anyone who writes letters. So, I'm sending this to your e-mail address through the school district's website link. Second, I can't use harsh or crude language that would tell you what I really think about school, so whatever you read in this e-mail needs to be multiplied by two or three to get the real impact of my opinion.

I hated high school. I absolutely hated high school. My friends hated high school. During our junior year we began a countdown at 300 days until graduation. We figured we could endure anything for 300 days, but it was tough.

Why did I hate high school? Because the classes are so useless. Come on, do you ever use algebra, geometry, or calculus? When you pay your bills each month you use elementary school or middle school math, right, but we had to take all of those fancy, hard math classes that nobody could show any real use for.

We had to take three science classes in high school. Why? Do you use biology, chemistry, and physics at your job? Probably not.

We took English classes every year in high school just like we did in middle school. There's nothing new in English or language arts that any teacher ever showed me. Have you ever read those literature books we use? They are huge collections of ancient writings by people who mean nothing to me. Those same people probably mean nothing to you, but you made us read all of the poems, the short stories, the books, and the plays that get squeezed into those 1,000-page monster literature books. I'm perfectly willing to read anything that makes sense to me and that matters to me. Have you considered books like that? You know, books with a purpose I relate to.

Year after year we took social studies classes, civics, geography, world history, United States government, psychology, and sociology. Wouldn't we learn more if we read today's newspaper and figured out what to do about events that are happening now? Couldn't those social studies classes become more real to students by showing us how people in history had ideas or experiences that we could apply in our lives? When do you use your knowledge of world history?

By the senior year there was almost nothing left to do. If high school can be completed in three years, just let people graduate then.

Okay, I did like being in the concert band and in the jazz band. I love music. I've played trumpet since I was in the fifth grade. I taught myself how to play drums. Our band classes were great. I even paid attention when we learned about famous composers of great symphonies because their lives were amazing or were crazy or were not what I expected. I learned about the history of music because it was so cool and because I'm interested in it. Plus our jazz band recorded a CD of our favorite songs and we sold it all over town as well as on the school's website.

So, I hated high school for all the reasons I mentioned. I know a lot of other students who hate school or just put up with school but love music or sports or theater or some club. I guess we love what interests us. Except for music, nothing in high school ever interested me.

Thanks for reading this,
Brian Nicholas

Dear School Board Members,

My best memories of school are from elementary school. Everything was new, everything was exciting, and the whole place seemed so bright and colorful and like home. Teachers in elementary school made us work but also gave us time to draw and play and create things. We had to learn to read and write, but the teachers always found ways to make reading and writing into a game or at least I remember it that way. Teachers in elementary school always listened to us tell them about our birthday or our pet fish or something else.

Middle school and high school were really different from elementary school. High school classes were a rerun of middle school classes only with lots, lots, lots more reading, writing, and homework. I'm sure that I could have finished middle school in two years instead of three years. Seventh and eighth grades were pretty much the same thing, so why do it twice?

High school was okay, but nothing great. We sure did have a huge stack of textbooks to carry around. They all seemed pretty much alike. I really liked the teachers who did different things in class. I learned more with hands-on activities. Science experiments were cool. Using art was something I really liked. When I got to make a poster or a drawing to show what I had learned, I worked harder on it. Not many teachers let me do that, but the ones who did were my favorites.

I drew a poster once for my journalism class. It was designed to be a full-page advertisement in a newspaper. It listed on the left side the ingredients of some junk foods like soft drinks and chips. On the right side it listed the ingredients of our algebra II book and our literature book. The left column headline was empty calories. The right column headline was empty ideas. The teacher disagreed with my opinion, but I got an A on the project because I did everything I was required to. When the students in class listened to my presentation about my advertisement, they cheered.

I guess you want me to tell you an idea for improving school. Okay, here's my idea—don't wait until after students graduate from high school to get their opinions about school.

Thanks,
Robert Alexander

⚜

Dear School Board Members,

Thank you for coming to our high school graduation. Thank you for sending me a letter of congratulations. Thank you for asking my opinion about school. I have a lot of opinions.

The school buildings are in bad shape. Anyplace I go to shop is in much better condition. Every restaurant in town is cleaner than our cafeterias. Are the bathrooms at school ever cleaned? Why does the heater come on in September and the air conditioning come on in February?

There are criminals at my old high school. Some students are criminals at school and away from school. You know who they are. Get them out of school so everyone else can be safe.

Do you have any idea how many people who are on free lunch lied about that? I've seen students with cell phones and cars getting free lunch. Some of those same students steal at school or cheat on tests. Can't you do something about that?

Why do you serve breakfast at school? My first period class always had three students showing up late because they took their sweet time at breakfast. Are we a school or a fast-food restaurant?

Okay, you probably want to know what I think of my classes. I liked most of my high school classes. Middle school was such a waste. Sixth grade was a review of fourth and fifth grade. All we heard in seventh and eighth grade was that we needed to work hard to get ready for high school. Why not just go on to high school?

High school classes were okay. A few were really boring, but nobody complained because they were so easy. I usually made a C or B in the boring classes, even though they were easy. They were more boring than they were easy so I just did enough to get by or to help my grade point average stay above the requirement to be on the swim team.

I had one very hard class each year in high school. I always made an A or a B in these classes. They were hard, but the teachers were so excited about what they taught that I took it seriously and worked extra.

The best classes in high school were with teachers who were superserious about teaching but really liked students and gave us all kinds of different things to do. I made straight A grades in those classes.

So my advice is that you fix up the school buildings, clean up the school buildings, lock up the students who are criminals, do something about middle school so it is worth three years of my life and get more high school teachers to be more excited and, you know, creative in how they teach.

Sincerely,
Laura Robertson

⚜

Dear School Board Members,
Just a quick e-mail to say thanks but no thanks. I'm a high school graduate now. School is over. I'm out. I have no desire to think about school. For thirteen years I did what everyone at school made me do. I'm free now.

Ask Ms. Richmond about me if you need to know more. She's the high school Spanish teacher I had for four years of Spanish. Most teachers just put up with me. Ms. Richmond took the time to get to know me. I did my best work in her classes. Her classroom was like going to Mexico or Spain or South America. It

was so real. The other classes were anything but real. My advice—have Ms. Rich-
mond teach the other teachers how to teach.

Adios,
Bob Anderson

＊

Dear School Board Members,
I wish I had more time to give you a much longer answer, but I'm really busy with
a job I just started and summer school college classes I'm taking to get an early
start on my freshman year of college.

The only thought I would share with you is to cut back on all of the writing in
every middle school class and in every high school class. Something must have
happened that made every teacher give us endless writing projects. We wrote in
science, math, English, history, art, computer, health, physical education, drama,
statistics, biology, sociology, and everything else.

My high school physical education teacher was great at organizing active
games or sports for us, but he hated to take time away from physical activity for
us to sit down and write. Actually, the writing in P.E. class was almost interesting
when we wrote about soccer rules because I played on the school's soccer team,
but I had never given much thought to why the rules are like they are or to how a
soccer referee watches a soccer game.

Anyway, we did way too much writing in all of our classes. Who decided that writ-
ing is what every student should do in every class? What was that decision based on?

Sincerely,
Kelly Walling

＊

Dear School Board Members,
I think it was in my ninth grade language arts class that we read some poem or
short story or book that made a statement about "what might have been." When
I think about school I always think about what might have been.

My best teacher was my tenth grade world history teacher. He would have been
my eleventh grade U.S. history teacher, but he left our school to go work in another
school system because he had to make more money for his family. What might have
been learned in an eleventh grade history class if that teacher had taught it instead
of three terrible teachers we had? The first one quit. The second one quit. The third
one should have quit, but even though she was the worst, she stayed the longest.

What might have been if the budget for band and orchestra had not been cut? If the arts and humanities classes had not been eliminated? If the speech team had a coach as good as the basketball team's coach was for that group?

What might have been learned in science classes at my high school if our science labs were as good as the science labs at the new high school? Same with computers, ours are old and slow. Theirs are new and hyperfast.

But, even if all of the building changes could be made, what might have been if you had removed those twenty-five or so students who kept everyone from feeling safe at school and always disrupted class.

What might have been if the teachers who were just putting in their time until retirement had actually done their job better? Or if those teachers who were always absent on Friday or Monday to give themselves a long weekend had been at school to give us a better education.

When I think of school, I think of what might have been.

Sadly,
Debra Rammer

⌖

Dear School Board Members,
As you know, I just graduated from Mission View High School. The school opened my ninth grade year so I'm in the first class that went to the school for four years. It is a great school. The building is good but nothing superfancy. The school schedule is pretty typical for high schools with four block periods per day and then four different classes the next day. We have all kinds of sports and clubs and activities. Most students who just graduated will start college soon, but many other students are either starting a job, going into the military, or entering a vocational program. Some are not just entering a vocational school, they are continuing vocational school with that new high school/vocational school partnership that guarantees a job when you complete the program.

The best part about our high school was that during the spring of our eighth grade year, we came to the high school for a full day and created our individual four-year plan for high school. I updated and improved my plan each year in high school at the annual meeting with my counselor and my teacher-mentor. I just always felt like the teachers and everyone else knew each student. It made school feel like a team or a family. I wondered sometimes how Mission View High School did that. I hope you will find out exactly how they did that and be sure that continues.

Thanks very much,
Matthew Brockman

⌖

Those letters from high school students to their school board are based on real comments that high school students have shared with me in recent years when I asked them how high school was going. The typical answer is "okay" followed by details about one outstanding teacher, success stories from one fantastic extracurricular activity, and several "you know, it's school, it's just school" comments about enduring the rest of the routine, especially classes that are quite ordinary. The high school students with whom I have spoken are cordial, capable, cooperative, reasonable teenagers who are quite willing to increase the effort they make in their high school classes. They are ready to become extreme students when they are challenged, inspired, nurtured, encouraged, and convinced that their increased effort is justified. In an occasional class or in an occasional extracurricular activity they demand of themselves total effort, total commitment, and superior results. If what is done with, for, and to those students in part of school were done in all of school, there would be no more regrets about what might have been.

It concerns me to hear so many high school students comment that overall school is nothing more than okay. We know what great high school teachers do to challenge students, inspire students, effectively teach students to cause learning by students. We know the same about middle school and elementary school. The missed opportunities and the regrets of "what might have been" are unacceptable. How do we go from "what might have been" to "what can be"? The answers begin as we hear from some teachers who are also writing to school board members.

Dear School Board Members,

I don't want to be completely negative, so I'll start by saying thank you for the friendly letter you sent to all teachers as you expressed your appreciation for our hard work during the school year. I really wish that it had been a better school year. I was so ready when the students arrived in August, but by December I was exhausted and by April I wondered how I would finish the year. I've always loved being a teacher. It is the only job that ever interested me, but the past few years have been so difficult that I wonder how long I can continue.

Bless their hearts, many of my students want to learn, but they get so little of my time and effort because of students who are failing and those who are misbehaving. How did so many students get to ninth grade without knowing how to read well, how to write well, how to behave in a classroom, or how to speak to adults? I call their parents and guardians. Some of the families help, others never return a phone call or attend a meeting at school. Our school social worker went to the home to get one mother to come to school. The mother came and started a big argument in the office. You expect us to be friendly to visitors, right? How do you continue to be friendly when you are verbally abused by a belligerent parent? When that parent met with me I heard endless excuses from her. We got nowhere. Her son still misbehaves, still lies, steals, cheats, and disrupts class. That is what I deal with daily. The boy fully cooperated one day, which was when the college basketball player visited our school for an assembly and then came to my classroom. I can't get a college athlete to come each day to help control that student so what am I supposed to do?

I just keep wondering what might have been learned by the many students who want to learn or at least will cooperate with me if I did not have to be a classroom law enforcement officer instead of a teacher. I even think I could get those defiant students to do some work, but it would take another person to help me or I would need to work with those students in a smaller group.

One more thought. Please come visit my classroom and many other classrooms. I know you hear a lot of reports and presentations at your school board meetings, but if you want to know what reality is at school you need to come see for yourself.

Thank you,
Christy James

Dear School Board Members,
Thank you for writing to all of the teachers. I know it was a form letter generated by a computer, but it was still a thoughtful expression, or was it?

Here's my point. I cannot teach my students by using form letters generated by a computer. I am expected to make every student a school superstar. The leaders of this school district keep telling me to get to know my students. Well that's about like you trying to get to know all of the teachers. Your form letter sent to me and my short response to you really don't give us much getting-to-know-you time together. That's my real point—there just is not enough time in a teacher's day to complete every responsibility you expect us to complete.

Here's my idea—please come be a substitute teacher for a few days. Come do my job and then you can tell me how I can improve the way I do my job. Come show me ways that I can save time, be more efficient, be more productive, and keep up with every new duty that gets added to my constantly expanding list of responsibilities.

I always thought I was a good teacher, but the job has changed so much that it makes me wonder. How can anyone, even the greatest teacher, get sixteen hours of work done in ten hours of time each day?

Please visit,
Marty Lebanon

Dear School Board Members,

This responds to your recent letter. I do appreciate your encouraging words. I agree that our school district has many outstanding teachers who are dedicated to their students. I'd like to think that I am one of those high-quality teachers.

I need you to know that I hear very discouraging comments from many teachers. They keep saying that more and more students just don't work very hard at school. Homework is barely done or is not done by more and more students are other common concerns. Teachers tell me that they just resort to having students read the textbook in class and do worksheets in class because it usually keeps people quiet and at least they can supervise the students to be sure the work gets done by everyone without copying off another student's paper. They say that most students barely read any reading assignment given as homework.

I had some problems like that at the start of the school year so I just casually confronted the students. I asked them, "Why are so many of you not doing the homework?" They were equally direct and blunt. Their answers can be summarized with two ideas. First, they said that the homework assignments were just more of the same old school stuff. Second, they said a homework assignment made one day and due at the next class was impossible with all of their other classes, school activities, part-time jobs, family demands on their time, church youth group, music lessons, weekend activities, and more.

We agreed that homework assignments would be different from the same old school stuff they were tired of and that they would have one week notice on all homework assignments. It worked.

I'll bet that lots of teachers have figured out great solutions to other problems in schools. What can you do to help set up ways for teachers to communicate good ideas?

Thanks,
Kimberly McLane

❖

Dear School Board Members,

It was so good to receive your letter. Of course, I hoped it would include a bonus for all of that good work you thanked us for, but it was still encouraging to read your friendly words.

You asked me to tell you what I am concerned about at school. I'm concerned about smart students who are not being challenged to use their brain to its complete potential. We do so much for failing students, for struggling students, and for students who have a learning disability or some other special needs condition. We need to keep doing all of that. We also need to challenge and support our most capable students. It's wrong to assume that since they are smart they will be fine on their own. They deserve the best just like the other students do.

Sincerely,
John Mitchell

⁜

Dear School Board Members,
Are you sure you want my ideas? I think about school a lot so my letter might be longer than you expected, but you did ask, so here goes.

It bothers me that some teachers arrive late, leave early, and complain about students who arrive late to class and skip class. Setting a good example can be effective.

It concerns me that some students seem to think that all they have to do at school is eat breakfast, eat lunch, and threaten to call their mother or their lawyer if anyone tells them what to do.

I get tired of adults who make excuses for students. Parents or guardians are just enabling their children when they make excuses for them.

I get sick of faculty meetings or any other meeting that could have been done just as well with e-mail. My time is precious. Don't waste my time at an unnecessary meeting.

I get concerned about gossip I hear in the faculty lounge so I rarely go in there. How can people talk, talk, talk about students or about the school district and then never do anything that really helps?

Is there anything we can do about students who are absent a lot for no valid reason? Is there anything we can do about teachers and other school employees who are absent a lot with no valid reason?

Is there some way you could convince the federal government to leave us alone to do our job? Does anyone think that bureaucrats and politicians in Washington, D.C., can make schools in every part of the country better even though every school is unique?

Could you stop the "new idea of the year" each year? In August of each year we are told what this year's new quick fix for education will be. Let's just do what we know works.

My biggest concern is students who always make C grades. They are stuck in the average category. They see themselves as average. They never qualify for any program that helps failing students or challenges talented students.

Thanks for reading my letter. Let me know what I can do to help.

Thanks,
Andrew Phoenix

⁜

Dear School Board Members,

Thanks for your letter. It's taken me a few days to reply because, to be honest, I was tired, actually exhausted, when the school year ended. In recent years I just stay exhausted all during the school year. I do my job well, but you and everyone else tell us to do more each year. I cannot get up in the morning any earlier and I cannot stay up at night any later. I can't stay exhausted all the time either. Something has to change.

I love my job. I love to teach. But I can't let this kill me. My family deserves more of my time than they get. My wife and children deserve a husband and a father who is not worn out every night. Something has to give. You have to show me ways to do this job and have a life away from the job.

I asked my principal and assistant principal for advice and help. They said it was the same for them. Can you believe this—forty years ago our school had a principal and assistant principal. School administration is much more complex and demanding and time-consuming now than it was forty years ago, but our school still has one principal and one assistant principal. No other organization in the country has the same management structure today that it had forty years ago. Something has to change.

Sometimes it seems that people who make decisions about education—school board members, governors, state legislators, Congress, or the president—want to be helpful but end up making things worse. You need to visit schools and you need to keep in touch with people who work at schools so you can base your decisions on reality.

One more comment. In recent years teachers have had pay raises of 1 percent or 2 percent. Do you think that will attract the best college students to enter the teaching profession? Do you think that will financially enable teachers to stay in this profession? Are you getting 1 percent or 2 percent salary increases in your job?

Sincerely,
Jack Welch

Some of the issues raised by the students and teachers in their letters to the school board are broad societal matters over which schools have no direct authority but which impact the schools. When family structures change, the students in those families bring to school the complexities and the difficulties of challenging family issues.

Some of the topics mentioned by the students and teachers are under the jurisdiction of elected political leaders, school superintendents, principals, or a school's governing body if decentralized decision-making processes have given certain powers to school councils. The processes, time, frustrations, meetings, compromises often involved with resolving issues through legislation or policy push the limits of endurance but can contribute to progress.

The issues that students and teachers can directly impact relate to what happens in classrooms. Teachers have much freedom in the classroom to select from a long list of options as they design lessons for students. Among those options is to design meaningful, fascinating, interactive, challenging class activities that will gain the commitment of students, cause learning, and build a classroom learning community in which the teacher and the students learn with and from one another. When that is done, what type of letter might a student or a teacher write to tell school board members about their classroom experiences?

Dear School Board Members,

By the time I was a high school senior my class schedule was not much to get excited about. Senior English class was required. My parents insisted that I keep taking math and science, so I signed up for calculus and physics. My girlfriend is interested in politics, so we got in the same U.S. government class. I like Spanish so I got in a Spanish IV class. Journalism looked interesting. Speech and drama would be easy I thought, but I was wrong. It was a good class but really hard work. So, I had one more class to take and what was available? Not much. My school counselor suggested life skills, which used to be called home economics. I figured, why not, so I signed up for it.

Life skills is so cool. It's a great class. I can't believe I liked it so much and learned so much. I thought it would be a boring, easy A grade and that I could get homework done for other classes while the life skills teacher lectured about how to be a good baby-sitter or how to organize the weekly grocery shopping. Wrong.

The first day of class began with the teacher asking us about our favorite snacks. We listed lots of junk food like chips and soft drinks and stuff like that. She knew what our answers would be so she brings out real samples of those foods. Then she really surprises us. The vocational education automobile engineering teacher loaned our life skills teacher an old, nasty car battery. The life skills teacher, Ms. Kelwin, pours my favorite soft drink on the old car battery and in no time all of the dirty corrosion is coming off the battery. Everyone laughed until she asked, "If it does that to built-up car battery residue, what is it doing in your stomach?" We were speechless. From that day on I've been loyal to bottled water and no hip, cool, neat, fun, celebrity-endorsed soft drink can get me to change my mind.

Every high school student wants to look good, right. We want to wear the cool clothes. So, Ms. Kelwin has this clothing designer who was in her life skills class ten years ago come talk to us about the work she does. She designs clothes and some of us wear clothes she has designed. She told us that she plans to create her own design company. She also said that her career dreams and plans began ten years ago when she was a student in Ms. Kelwin's class. She designed a new color or shade of a color for her recent spring fashion line and she calls the new color "Kelwin" and has ads encouraging people to dress to be a Kelwinner. Isn't that neat?

So, life skills was a great class. Everything in it related to high school students. We had tons of work to do for the class, but everyone did the work because it was interesting. I'll admit that the research I had to do about how clothing manufacturers use chemistry in the development of fabrics seemed weird at first. Then it made sense. It was really the first time I had seen much use for chemistry.

In March Ms. Kelwin told us that our biggest project of the year would be due on May 10, right in the middle of Senior prom and graduation season. Our class would plan and present a wedding. It was like starting a business. There was so much to do. Ms. Kelwin gave us a budget of $12,000 and we thought that was a fortune. After we got prices for dresses, flowers, cake, invitations, rings, tuxedos, reception, rehearsal dinner, limousine, and honeymoon we thought the budget was impossible, but we made it work. I was the best man in the wedding. My girlfriend was one of the bridesmaids so that was really cool.

So, I thought you would like to know that life skills is a great class. Please be sure that schools keep that class and tell students about life skills. I almost missed out on that class. Be sure to take great care of Ms. Kelwin. She is a fantastic teacher. She could probably make lots more money doing other work. Please do whatever it takes to keep her at my high school.

Thanks,
Ken Johnson

⚜

Dear School Board Members,
I'm honored that you asked for my ideas. I appreciate your letter. It was perfectly timed. I just taught the most amazing class and I would like you to know all about it.

My teaching certification includes several categories. I am certified to teach art in grades kindergarten through high school, reading in grades six through twelve, social studies in grades six through twelve, plus I am certified to be a principal in middle school or high school. I intend to be a teacher throughout my career, but the right administrative opportunity may open up someday and I wanted to be prepared for that.

Our school decided to begin a humanities class for tenth or eleventh graders. The class would be a liberal arts collection of many subjects ranging from music to art, from dance to creative writing, from the history or works of artists and composers and writers to the most modern use of technology in creative endeavors such as animation or concerts. I agreed to teach the class and to create the curriculum for it.

Students knew that this humanities class was a requirement, so they accepted it or reluctantly put up with the reality of another requirement. I was determined to make this a class the students would learn in and would long remember. So in May, a few months before the class would start in August, I asked a lot of ninth and tenth graders for ideas about what would make this a great class. First they asked me what "humanities" meant. Good question. I told them that it included everything from music to philosophy, from art to literature, from dance to movies. They still thought humanities was a strange word to communicate the neat activities of music or movies. We began calling it a new name. The students kept using the word creative to describe what the class seemed to be about. They were concerned that the class might just be a review of what other artists, writers, or performers many years ago did that was seen as creative. So, we called the class "creative opportunities for original learning," which we nicknamed COOL with its acronym. The different attitudes that can be created when students get to take a COOL class instead of having to take a required humanities class are amazing. From the start I was determined to use student input in designing and implementing the class.

To make a long story short, the students loved the class and did outstanding, brilliant work. Our study of music went from Beethoven to the Beatles to Broadway to currently popular performers I had never heard of, but which the students were experts on. Our study of creative writing and philosophy ranged from Plato to websites, from Emerson to Martin Luther King Jr., from Dr. Seuss to science fiction. Dance ranged from ancient tribal ceremonies to nineteenth-century groups such as the Shakers, from square dancing to ballroom dancing, from how their parents/guardians danced to how students now dance. We thoroughly analyzed the sociology, psychology, history, economics, and other connections with each topic or activity. There was never a dull moment in class.

I kept myself open to spontaneous opportunities. The curriculum was very clear and very specific, but how that curriculum was taught was wisely left open. When a big concert at a local arena impressed students, we would research the economics of staging a massive concert for 20,000 people to attend. Then we would contrast that with how the ancient Greeks staged theatrical performances.

So, I hope you will come visit my COOL class next year. I know what the students will learn, but I don't now exactly how next year's students will learn it. That's part of what intrigues and inspires me about teaching. Please never do anything that would limit the amazing experiences we can have in classrooms when we are free to create and invent what works with our students.

Respectfully,
Marian Nelson

There is hope. The life skills and humanities classes offer ideas and insights about how to make the classroom experience meaningful, productive, fascinating, and rewarding for students and teachers.

Notice closely the symbiotic results in the life skills class and in the humanities class. Students and teachers had valuable experiences that produced much learning and mutual commitment. The students learned about life skills and humanities. The teachers learned about how their current students learn, and that enabled the teachers to learn more about teaching. The students connected life skills and humanities with their prior knowledge and current interests to build new talents, understanding, skill, ability to learn more, eagerness, and curiosity to learn more.

Many complicated issues confront education today. That will be true tomorrow, next year, and forever. Despite those complications, within a classroom abundant learning can occur. Perhaps we cannot prevent the complications of tight budgets, federal government interference, or the issue of the moment, but we can go into our classrooms and cause learning.

Extreme teachers can cause extreme learning in the lives of extreme students. No matter what complications, difficulties, complexities, and problems surround the classroom, quality learning can occur within the classroom. Is this attitude optimistic? Yes. Is this conclusion realistic? Yes, great teaching occurs in schools daily. Is this perspective important? Yes, students deserve the best possible education and in providing that exemplary education, teachers have the best possible education career.

We can condemn the sources of problems in education or we can create the solutions to the extent that our authority permits. For teachers, the authority to cause learning is virtually unlimited. When teachers do all they can with the students in their classrooms, the results can be extreme. The students deserve that extreme learning experience and they can respond favorably to extreme learning experiences. Their enthusiastic response can be an essential step toward becoming extreme students. We will now consider the characteristics of extreme students as we also begin investigating the educational environment in which extreme students thrive.

Is this really possible? Sure. The life skills students and the humanities students experienced extreme learning as made possible by their extreme teachers. Those students began to feel, sense, think, and know what it is like and why it is worth it to be extreme students. Possible? Of course. Easy? No. Important, rewarding, and worth it? Absolutely! For students and for teachers.

Chapter 3

Characteristics of Extreme Students

The students in my classes are taught according to the extreme teaching research, methods, concepts and wide-open, unlimited possibilities. As a result, students master the curriculum requirements; make good grades; commit themselves to do the work that academic achievement requires; become enthusiastic about class; cooperate with their teacher to build a learning community; succeed; attain a depth of knowing that includes understanding; recall information but also think, analyze, explain, and apply; master the basics but advance far beyond that basic mastery; and successfully experience extreme learning, which has a depth, width, length, application, relevance, fascination, and challenge that inspires a curiosity to learn more. That wholesome curiosity for intellectual knowledge is a fundamental characteristic of extreme students.

One question should be resolved and removed at the outset: Are extreme students made or born? My operating principle is that almost every student can be an extreme student who has a wholesome intellectual curiosity for knowledge. If the young scholar comes to my classroom as an extreme student it is my duty to fully nurture, challenge, develop, and inspire that experienced, extreme student so his or her wholesome intellectual curiosity for knowledge is continually functioning, expanding, achieving, and producing. If a middle school, high school, college, or graduate school student comes to my classroom and has not yet become a practicing extreme student, my responsibility has two parts. First, the student must become so absolutely fascinated with the learning experiences in our class that he or she commits to a new level of academic achievement. Second, having inspired, disturbed, energized, and awakened the latent abilities of this student, I must now fully nurture, challenge, develop, and inspire that new extreme student so his or her newfound wholesome intellectual curiosity for knowledge is continually supported, sustained, encouraged, acknowledged, and worthwhile so the new extreme student joins the ranks of the permanent extreme students. Other people can debate the made or born question. My duty and my adventure is to do the work and reach the goals listed above for experienced extreme students and for new extreme students.

In 1995, when I conducted the research that provided the findings which became the foundation, premise, direction, and inspiration for three books—*High-Impact Teaching*, *Extreme Teaching*, and *Extreme Learning*—the research emphasized gaining insights about what great teachers do that makes them effective, memorable, and superior. The original findings have been confirmed repeatedly. Great teachers do the following:

1. Use a variety of teaching methods and activities
2. Are enthusiastic about teaching, about students, and about learning
3. Challenge their students
4. Connect learning today with the real lives of students now

My research curiosity then moved to the topic of great students. I sought insights about what great students do, how great students learn, how great students are motivated, what great students expect of themselves, and the actions that teachers can take to create a classroom environment filled with learning activities that create, inspire, nurture, and challenge great students. Responses to my surveys provided convincing evidence that the characteristics, traits, work ethic, attitude, and tendencies of great students can be clearly identified.

Very successful students, those whom I call extreme students, are not only the young scholars who are identified as gifted and talented, although many of those students do become extreme students and probably all of those students could become extreme students.

A student who is doing poorly in school, a student who is getting by with a C average or passing with a D average, a student who easily makes the honor roll yet rarely seriously pushes himself or herself to do challenging work because most of school comes so easily, these students and others can become extreme students.

The research findings about very successful students tell us that extreme students have these characteristics:

1. Extreme students have a wholesome intellectual curiosity for knowledge. They are curious in a healthy, lively, purposeful way. They can thrive in school when their curiosities are connected with what they are learning. They may dismiss school as not worth much effort if their curiosities are not applied, are not developed, are not connected to school subjects and classes. They may accept from themselves far less than their best work if school becomes a routine of ordinary activities and redundant procedures. The words "curious" and "inquisitive" were mentioned most often in the research.
2. Extreme students ask questions. They are encouraged to ask questions. Their questions are taken seriously, which makes more students comfort-

able and confident about asking questions or about taking the risk of asking a question. Their questions and responses to those questions become part of the body of knowledge in the classroom. Their questions and the atmosphere in which they feel comfortable about and encouraged to ask questions or respond to questions help establish a student and teacher partnership, a classroom learning community.

3. Extreme students are active within their own minds. They think, wonder, explore, analyze. They are given classroom activities and assignments at school as well as family activities, duties, and opportunities at home or in the community, which exercise, develop, and apply their eagerness to think, wonder, explore, and analyze. Some respondents in the research indicated that they always had the personal drive to be an extreme student. Other respondents said that the effort of a teacher, family member, or community member guided, encouraged, and activated their effort, which led them to become an extreme student. The research indicated convincingly that a caring, capable, determined adult can appeal to the inherent characteristic of children and teenagers to be active within their own minds, to think, wonder, question, probe ideas, ask why, innovate, imagine, and create. The research findings also emphasized the impact of sacrifices adults made for a child or teenager. Several research respondents expressed intense emotional appreciation of and love for the adults whose sacrifices of time, money, personal ambition, or personal pleasure were made to support the curiosities, interests, dreams, and ambitions of an emerging extreme student.

4. Extreme students are organized. They manage time, materials, priorities, their behavior, and their pursuit of important goals with mature skills. These skills can be learned even if a person is not naturally inclined to be efficient and organized.

5. Extreme students read, read, and read.

6. Extreme students pay attention with total concentration. When reading, these students anticipate the ideas or the action of the next page. In class, these students listen intently, anticipate the next question, and create an internal conversation through which they teach themselves.

7. Extreme students work hard.

For readers who realistically and honestly question my optimism that extreme students can be the norm in school, I would suggest that in parts of life away from school children and teenagers are extreme in many activities. From participation in a neighborhood soccer league to involvement in a church youth group's mission trip to Central America, from starting a lemonade stand to make money in the summer to completing an Eagle Scout requirement of community service, from completely analyzing and mastering a new video game to completely analyzing statistics from professional sports teams, from understanding all of the features on computers, cell phones, or other technology applications to listening with awe as a grandparent tells her grandson stories about what the grandson's mother was like as a child, children and teenagers are inherently extreme. The process, the routines, and continual repetition of the ordinary activities at school unfortunately can de-extreme the vibrant wholesome intellectual curiosity for knowledge of some students. That is unacceptable.

For readers who realistically and honestly ask, "How do you know if these students are learning when they do all of these creative activities in classes? Do they ever have a pencil and paper test?"

One answer to that question is that extreme teachers also display characteristics of extreme students. I pay attention to what the students say in class discussions and that gives me a continuous measurement of their learning. I listen closely to their questions so I know how to answer and so I realize what their question tells me about what they have learned and about what they need to learn.

I give precise scoring guides with each homework project. The students know precisely what is expected and they often surpass the highest level of the scoring guide.

I give tests, pencil and paper tests. I create the tests to measure learning, apply/extend learning, and cause new learning. As I grade tests, I am also evaluating myself and seeing what I taught most effectively, what needs to be taught better, and which students need some individualized reteaching.

We do a lot of one- to five-minute drill and practice, recall, memory activities in class. We master the basics in traditional or innovative ways, but always with much enthusiasm.

Verbatim comments from the research provide strong statements and strong convictions to support the importance of creating, nurturing, challenging, developing, and encouraging extreme students.

Participants in this research represent a vast range of adults whose careers vary from physician to politics, engineering to economic development, community agency management to law enforcement, nurse to real estate, dentist to teacher, corporate management to school administration, stay-at-home mom to stay-at-home dad.

The survey's first question made the following request of respondents:

Please think of the greatest successes you had in school—elementary school, middle school or high school. Maybe it was the highest grade you ever made or the best paper you ever wrote. Maybe it was the most difficult challenge you encountered and mastered. Here are the questions: a) What did you do to create your success? Even if someone else motivated you or guided you, think about what you did to make the success happen; b) Now, think about what someone else did to support, encourage, guide or motivate you in this success. What did they do?

Some responses to part a—think about what you did to make this success happen—follow.

"My own competitiveness—wanting to be the best."

"I worked hard—I put forth a lot of effort."

"I stepped out of my comfort zone and attempted a personal challenge."

"I put in the necessary extra time to work on my goal."

"I quit listening to the little voice in my head that said, 'I can't' and I began to take control of my destiny."

"I studied long and hard, I listened in class, I took notes, and I participated in class discussions."

"I was resourceful. If I didn't understand a concept or how to do something, I found someone who did know and could help me. I was organized and planned time for studying and working on projects."

"I put forth 100 percent effort because I had a strong desire to achieve at the level the teacher had set for me."

"I diligently completed all assignments including extra credit. I asked questions and worked ahead of class."

"I paid attention and did the work."

"I paced myself. I was aware of deadlines and of the bottom line."

"I set a goal for myself—what I wanted to achieve by the end of the semester, which was an A in the class. I then looked at each step along the path as a key to the end."

"I took notes in class written in a way that I would understand them even if they were different words from what the teacher said exactly. Then I would read my notes often to keep understanding everything better."

"I listened. I participated in class discussions. I talked to other people about the subject outside of class."

"I decided to not procrastinate any more. I did all the work and I turned it in on time."

"I realized that I could be smart and popular, so I became as smart as I could and I still had lots of good friends."

"That's easy. I quit goofing off. I managed time so I got work done first and then I had free time left over."

Verbatim comments from the research provide precise, personal insight into the supportive role that other people played in the successes itemized above. These research responses are to the statement, "Now, think about what someone else did to support, encourage, guide, or motivate you in this success."

"Showing up at my school events let me know that my parents valued me and wanted me to succeed."

"My professor went out of his way to talk to me individually about my 'giftedness' for writing. He identified and affirmed for me a talent I did not know I had."

"They gave me confidence by showing their confidence in my abilities. They provided continuous, timely encouragement. They helped me see what hidden talents I possessed then encouraged me to develop them. They were always there for me."

"My mother saw education as my greatest hope. She supported me in every personal and resource way possible."

"They told me over and over again to believe in myself. They became irritated each time I tried to quit or put myself down. They were relentless in their encouragement, no matter what I felt or said."

"I remember my Spanish teacher sitting with me after school one day and helping me learn how to read the language for comprehension. It meant a lot that he believed in me. I think it contributed to my motivation to understand, not only for the grade."

"My teacher motivated me to want to study hard and make the A. He showed the relevance between the subject and the real world. He connected it to what was going on in my world."

"My parents and teachers were always proud of me and they let me know it. My self-motivation was ignited and guided by the verbal praise and recognition that I received from my teachers, parents and peers. Once you've been labeled a good student, it's hard to not always give 110 percent."

"My parents and teachers gave me opportunities to shine. They knew the things i could do well and they made sure I was given the chance to be successful. In the second grade I had been working hard on my handwriting skills and I was doing very well. One day, when I walked into the classroom, my teacher handed me the chalk and asked me to write the poem for the day on the chalkboard. She knew from my mom that I played school often and loved to write on the chalkboard. Wow, it felt great to be given the chance to do something that I knew I could do well."

"They showed me the potential I had and they wouldn't let me settle for less. They always set high standards."

"My mother and father both convinced me that I could do anything I wanted to do. That confidence made all the difference."

"They taught me what they knew, fully expecting me to master it."

"My parents have always instilled in me the 'you can do anything if you are willing to work at it' ethic."

"My mother was that constant push that kept letting me know that if I put my mind to it, I would do it."

Please notice how many of those helpful actions were in the categories of time, encouragement, support, being there, verbal statements of inspiration and pride, direct guidance, and concern. No laws, policies, or regulations can impact the amount of such human and humane actions. No laws, policies, or regulations can equal the favorable results that such human and humane actions can help produce.

Survey respondents were asked to think specifically about actions taken by very successful students—extreme students—which continually make them high achievers in school. Some of the verbatim responses follow, but first here's what the survey question stated: "Some students in schools consistently produce great results. They are very successful students year after year, class after class. What do these students do which makes them very successful students? Omit factors which are out of the control of a student such as genetics or family situations. Emphasize factors which students can control."

"Write down assignments and due dates. Start early on assignments rather than procrastinate."

"Concentrate in class to try to absorb the information."

"I always expected to get an A and was disappointed with anything less."

"Work hard. Invest effort. Contribute ideas. Complete assignments. Curiosity—want to know more and delve deeper."

"Work hard. Stay on task and stay focused. Read widely and beyond what's expected."

"Be prepared for class. Develop good listening skills and good note-taking skills. Finish tasks."

"Practice a lot. Dream big. Have a mentor to talk with and follow. Believe in yourself."

"Study consistently. Create a daily schedule that incorporates study time and quiet time."

"Learn how to learn. Persist even when the task gets difficult. Ask questions when you are unsure."

"Be organized. Stay positive. Ask how to do things better each time."

"Care about the quality of your work. Do all assignments thoroughly. Listen in class. Obey directions from teachers. Study."

"Take responsibility for learning. Be a curious, active participant in classes."

"Be on time, be prepared and be inquisitive. Challenge yourself by taking higher-level classes."

"Expect yourself and require yourself to turn in all work, study for tests, and earn higher grades."

"Complete all the work you are assigned to do no matter what it costs you in time and effort."

"Prepare in advance. Read ahead of the teacher. Want to learn more than what is offered."

"Ask why a lot. Engage in discussions with intelligent adults fearlessly."

"Look at everything as a step toward an end goal—nothing is useless or left out."

"Always on task, reading in any spare time, asking probing questions."
"Successful students expect to make an A on all assignments and be above
    grade level on all testing."

The survey respondents were asked a question that applied the methods of
learning to a setting away from school. How people learn and what motivates that
learning away from school can offer some perspective that is applicable at school.

"I see the benefit at work of knowing certain information and of having certain
    skills. I learn by reading books, talking to experienced workers and I learn
    by doing."
"I learned by interacting with people, reading, attending a conference and talk-
    ing to experts."
"I have other people evaluate and judge my work so I can learn from their ad-
    vice and feedback."
"I worked with mentors who helped me see my inner self—raw talents and
    abilities. I kept seeking out more people to help me."
"I am fascinated by cultures other than my own so I have cultivated friendships
    with people from other cultures."
"I wanted one thing in my life in which I would excel so I listened, observed,
    and practiced, practiced, practiced."
"My mother bought me a subscription to a kid's astronomy magazine. I
    thought it was cool to get mail, so I read it. The more I read, the more I
    wanted to learn. Now I could take a class, look up information on the Inter-
    net, join a club, and spend time viewing the starts and planets."
"I want to learn more about cooking. I could take a class, read more books, watch
    the cooking shows, practice more, talk with experts, and observe others."
"I am eager to learn because of my interest in the subject. I read and talk to
    people who know a lot. I research and go to seminars."
"An overall interest in the topic and some previous amateur success. I talked
    to others in the field, read, took a brief introductory class. I would like to
    take a very in-depth class I heard about."

The above comments endorse and confirm the motivating power of interest and
relevance. "I saw a benefit at work of knowing certain information" can remind
teachers that students may not see much benefit in their lives of what is to be
learned at school; however, when school learning connects with the wholesome
knowledge, talents, and interests of students, a dynamic change in attitude about
and commitment to school can occur. Some teachers may ask, "Why should I
have to make the curriculum connect with what students know, are interested in,
or are talented in? My teachers never did that for me. It's the curriculum. The students just have to learn it." I would respond by asking, "Why would you not take

full advantage of the benefits available from making connections between your curriculum and the students' wholesome knowledge, interests, and talents? Why deny yourself the use of that motivator for your students? Why deny yourself the experiences you could have with students who would eagerly interact with you and with the subject you teach if they saw that learning the subject connected with their real life right now? Why not use the wiring structure of the human brain, which is designed to make connections?"

The survey was designed to give respondents opportunities to include additional ideas that were specific or general. The survey respondents indicated that the time spent thinking about successful students and their personal motivations or methods to learn had been quite meaningful and revealing. The concluding section of the survey was welcomed as a way to offer ideas that the earlier portion of the survey had caused people to think about. Some of those survey responses follow.

"Most successful students have opportunities to pursue their own interests, learning through structured curriculum, but within a content subject matter of choice. Successful students learn more, also, as they share with others. Successful students have been given opportunities to discover and pursue unique interests and potential—a leading out, rather than a pouring in of learnings and discoveries."

"The common opinion among parents, teachers, and the public that innate ability or innate brilliance rather than hard work determines success is unfortunate for students and it lets teachers off the hook. Also, at the high school level the importance of an adult who cares needs emphasis."

"Successful students have connected the value of education to their future success."

"Successful students are focused on studies; turn in work on time; take books home to study; have a good balance of school, other duties including chores or a part-time job and personal time; don't look for ways to get out of work; have a close relationship with teachers to express ideas and to solve problems; and spend time with other motivated students."

"Successful students allow themselves to engage or to be engaged in learning."

"The most successful students are not only motivated by teachers, or self-motivated, but also are motivated by a positive support system of family, friends, and community."

"Students who care about their grades tend to get better grades."

"Successful students are curious, attentive, have a love of learning, have a positive attitude, are observant, are willing to work, and are goal oriented and are engaged in problem solving. Through completing this survey I came to believe that the most important thing is a love of learning, followed closely by a positive attitude."

"A successful student is really a student who enjoys the discovery process throughout his/her entire life."

Reading the survey responses many times and reflecting on the topic of extreme students, I developed a comprehensive perspective about characteristics of extreme students. Each student is unique and each extreme student is unique; however, some characteristics associated with becoming and being an extreme student do become clear. A summary follows.

Questions. Curiosities. Intellectual ambition. Academic hunger. Bold thoughts. Original ideas. Unique insights. Mental courage in a supporting environment to challenge the common, the superficial, the ordinary, the imposed boundaries, or the existing limits of thinking, learning, knowing, wondering, exploring, discovering, and asking. The relentless effort to know more, to understand deeply, to persist through difficulties or failures, to question eagerly, to explore the mind's frontier, the brain's fullness, and the infinity of thought. To combine a vibrant search for truth with an organized yet not fully predictable approach. To thirst for wisdom. To find meaning, purpose, and reward in the search for knowledge with inspiration coming both from the search itself and from the eventual knowledge gained. To realize that there is no limit to thinking. To learn, learn more, and keep learning. To have a wholesome intellectual curiosity for knowledge. To read, read more, and keep reading. To work, work more, and keep working, yet also have a variety of interests. To develop a healthy balance of priorities so you take care of heart, mind, body, and soul. This is to be an extreme student.

The research results describe, identify, and confirm the characteristics of extreme students. The research also indicated that extreme students thrive when given a supportive environment and an encouraging team of caring adults. We now turn our attention to creating the environment and the atmosphere in classrooms at schools in which extreme students are created, advised, nurtured, challenged, supported, taught, guided, and nourished.

Students benefit when they become extreme students and when their extremeness is encouraged, supported, guided, interacted with, taken seriously, and connected with their real lives right now. Teachers have a much more rewarding career experience when creating, developing, inspiring, nurturing, learning with, learning from, interacting with, challenging, and guiding extreme students.

Remember those letters in chapter 2 from students and teachers to school board members? One common idea throughout those letters can be put into the terminology of this book—please make school a place where extreme teachers cause extreme learning in the lives of extreme students and, reciprocally, in the lives of those teachers. The next chapter is designed to identify how an extreme classroom community is created so extreme students have the environment and atmosphere in which they thrive.

Chapter 4

Creating Conditions in Which Extreme Students Thrive

On the first day of a new school year, some students in elementary, middle, and high schools walk into their classrooms having already made the commitment and the decision to be extreme students. Teachers of these students have some demanding, important, and rewarding work to do. Those teachers need to fully challenge, encourage, guide, fascinate, and team up with the extreme students so the most productive, meaningful, and compelling learning activities are experienced.

On the first day of a new school year some students in elementary, middle, and high schools walk into their classrooms with moderate, minimal, or absolutely no commitment to learning at school, doing work at school, or cooperating at school. The optimistic attitude is that these students are not extreme students yet. The stark reality is that teachers of these students have some demanding and probably frustrating work to do; however, that work can be meaningful and rewarding as the teacher creates learning activities that persuade students to make a greater commitment to school. The "not extreme yet" students do have wholesome knowledge, interests, and talents that can be connected to what needs to be learned at school. The "not extreme yet" students have probably shown wholesome curiosities at some point in their life, but circumstances, failures, family problems, school being boring, distractions, or other factors have de-extremed these students in terms of a willingness to learn at school. For most "not extreme yet" students, activities and methods in classrooms can be designed and experienced to begin and eventually to complete the process of a "not extreme yet" student becoming an extreme student. It should be noted again that the approximately 5 percent of students with severe and repeated misbehavior at school and/or with a criminal record of offenses at school and/or in the community need to be educated in alternative programs. The alternative program can be much more effective for that 5 percent of the student population. Also, the other 95 percent of students deserve to be free from and protected from the students who are repeatedly and severely disruptive at school or are school/community criminals.

I can hear the question, so I'll ask it and answer it. "Shouldn't students accept their responsibility to do their school work? Isn't that just part of being a proper student? Why is it my job to challenge everyone and motivate everyone and to make fascinating mental connections between the curriculum and interests the students have? I'm the teacher. I have my education. Shouldn't students just do what they are supposed to do, you know, do what I tell them to do?"

The issue is, How can the learning experience for each student be fully challenging and meaningful? How can average or failing students be fascinated and inspired into working harder and learning more? Whether students come into the classroom eager, disciplined, and dedicated or whether students come into the classroom apathetic, effective teaching is needed and is possible.

If students are going to break their old habits of just working enough to pass, of comfortably making a C average, of getting good grades but not really working very hard, of doing well but being able to do much better, then some of the habitual learning experiences they are given need to be broken, changed, improved, discarded, or replaced. A better classroom environment, atmosphere, learning community, and work ethic can be established. What does it include? What does it look like and feel like? How does it change from day to day? What is constant from day to day or is everything subject to change? Let's answer those questions beginning with a series of student profiles.

Hi. My name is Taylor Mitchell. I have an identical twin sister, Samantha. I've always been glad that our parents gave us really different names. You cannot mistake the name Taylor for the name Samantha. You know, some families might choose matching names for twins like Ellen and Eileen or Mary and Carey. It's confusing enough for sisters to be absolutely identical in how they look, so at least Samantha and I have names that don't rhyme and are not spelled alike.

Samantha and I play on the girl's soccer team at our high school. We started playing soccer ten years ago when we were six years old. I actually started when I was five, but Samantha did not like soccer until I started to like it and then she just had to do what I was doing. That's okay. I play forward on our team so I'm supposed to lead the offense, take shots, set up shots for other players, get assists, and score goals. Samantha plays goalie which, I admit, is a tough job. Make a good save and you are the hero. Let a shot get past you into the goal and you feel awful plus people always think you should have stopped the shot from going in even though they could never do that themselves.

As for school, well, you know, it's school. I keep my grades way above the requirement to play sports, but I'm no superbrain who makes straight A grades and will get a scholarship to Harvard. I'll graduate in two more years and I'll have a 3.0 average or better. Most of my grades are B with an A here and a C there.

I really, really like my computer class. I even got involved with a technology club at school. My soccer friends tell me I'm going geek or nerd on them and that I'll get *lost in some computer virtual world and never escape. I tell them that some companies hire high school graduates to do technology work and pay $30,000 to start. Imagine me an eighteen-year-old just out of high school making that much money.*

My other classes are what you would expect. History, English, science, Spanish, math, math, and more math. What's the point of algebra, geometry, more algebra, and then calculus? Our computer teacher tells us how important algebra and calculus are for technology, but that's not the type of computer work I would ever do.

I do have this really cool chemistry class. I'm no scientist, but when the teacher brought in a baseball, a soccer ball, a basketball, a tennis racket, running shoes, a water ski, and a skateboard, that got my total attention. For a week or more we did experiments about the materials used to make those sporting goods and about the whole manufacturing process of producing those sports products. I was amazed. I learned a lot.

Most of my classes never do anything cool like the chemistry class does. We read all the time and we write forever. What's with all the writing? When I was in middle school our teachers told us they had to make us write more. It has never stopped. What's the big deal about writing? Nobody ever explained to me why it is such a good idea to write all the time.

So, school is okay. I like seeing my soccer friends. My grades are good enough. I really don't expect much; just let me play soccer and I'll be fine. Now Samantha is another story, so you should ask her about school.

⚜

Hey. I'm Samantha Mitchell. You already met my twin sister, Taylor. She's a great soccer player, I mean superstar. She can play college soccer if she is willing to make the effort. She's always been good at soccer, but my parents sent her to some soccer camps a few years ago and she's been a pro ever since. I work hard at soccer and I like it a lot. I went to goalie camp once in July three years ago, but just once. You know, in the summer I like to play tennis, swim, and make money baby-sitting. If I play soccer after high school it would just be for fun.

Now, about school. There are lots of students who are smarter than I am. You know, they just naturally have superbrains. My brains are pretty average, but I work hard, really hard. It's not that I'm excited about all of my classes, but I am determined to get a scholarship to pay for college. The president of a college that is about twenty miles from here spoke to my eighth grade class two years ago. He said that each year his college selects fifteen students from schools in this state to be given a full four-year scholarship to the college. I'm going to be one of those fifteen students who are selected in two years. So I work hard in classes, but only as hard as it takes to make an A, which in a lot of classes is not all that hard. I just ask students who had the same teacher for the same class last year what it takes to make an A. I do what they tell me, nothing more or less. It almost always works. I guess teachers never change what they do.

Next year I'll take physics and that bothers me. Whatever I end up doing with my life will have absolutely nothing to do with physics. I will not be an astronaut or a pilot. I will not be a technology wizard or an engineer. I've asked people what it takes to make an A in physics. They told me to memorize the physics book. Great. That will be such fun. Memorize the charts, graphs, and pages of that monster book. Maybe we'll get a new physics teacher next year.

So, that's pretty much what I think about school. You know what you should do? Talk to my little cousin, Jason. He's in seventh grade. He can tell you all about middle school. He's already in his third year of middle school so, get it, he flunked. He probably has a story to tell.

⁂

Hey, I'm Jason Phillips. I'm glad you met Taylor and Samantha. They are my favorite cousins. It's pretty cool being related to two great soccer players who also happen to be movie-star beautiful. You should see all the guys at the soccer games. It's like Taylor and Samantha are celebrities.

Anyway, yeah, I flunked sixth grade, but it was not all my fault. Sixth grade is so dull. I already knew everything we were doing. Everything. Teachers never expect much from me, but I've got ideas and all that, but who listens to my ideas? So, I did really well in elementary school and then sixth grade was just the same old stuff again. I got bored. I daydreamed. I goofed off. I did not do homework. I flunked. I passed sixth grade the second time because it was no fun being one year older than all of those little children who were sixth graders. I begged everybody to get me to skip to eighth grade. Not a chance.

Well, I got to seventh grade and my math teacher asks me to wait after class one day. She says something like, "Jason, you know all of this don't you? We've got to find a way to get you up to the eighth grade." Great idea. Sounds cool to me. She works out a contract so if I make all A and B grades the first semester of seventh grade and if I show I'm at eighth grade level on some fancy tests, plus if I never get in trouble, I can go to the eighth grade in January and get back where I belong. I agreed and so did my mom and stepfather. Guess what it's like at my house every night? My parents watch me constantly to be sure I am studying.

So, this math teacher decides that I'm not the only student in seventh grade who can do a lot more than the dumb daily stuff seventh graders in math usually do. She starts teaching us algebra and geometry and statistics. We use the gym at school to set up big geometry puzzles which she had a fancy word for, but puzzle is good enough. We did all kinds of math problems using statistics from professional and college sports. We analyzed some middle school volleyball and football games. The coaches were amazed when we showed them the results and why they were winning or losing games. The math is actually kind of neat because it is about sports. Math usually is just about dumb numbers, which I call dumbers instead of numbers. But now we call them statistics, which sounds all grown up and important.

So, I'll finish eighth grade easy. I'll go to high school on schedule with my friends, but I want to move through high school fast. I'm doing two years of middle school in one year, so why take four years to finish high school? I want to get out of school and go be a television sports show announcer using all of my sports statistics skills.

You remember I said how well I did in elementary school? Go talk to my neighbor, Andy. He's in fifth grade. He can tell you about elementary school.

⁂

Hello, I'm Andy. I'm in the fifth grade. I'm new at this school. That was tough. I had to make new friends, but most people already had friends. I did get to know Thomas and Rosa and Hunter. Hunter is a girl and she has a neat name which I really like. She has been friendly to me and everyone at school likes her. Thomas, Rosa, Hunter, and I play together at recess some days. We ride the same bus to school. We call each other sometimes at night or weekends.

I was so lost when I came to this school. My parents got divorced last summer. My mom and I moved from where my dad lives. Mom said we had to get away from that city. I cried a lot. I miss Dad and I miss my old friends. That's not fair.

I think a teacher asked Hunter to talk to me at recess. Teachers are like that, I guess, looking out for unhappy students. I think the teacher was Ms. Sullivan because she's nice. She teaches most of my classes except reading, art, music, and gym. For reading I go to Mr. Buckner, who has a room full of books and pictures and computers and stuff. Mr. Buckner called on me in class the first day and that was strange. Give the new guy some time would you? He says, "Andrew, I guess you prefer Andy." I nodded yes. "Andy, what's the best book you have read?" Everyone looks at me. I don't know what to say at first. Then I remember that at a Bible school activity two summers ago we read the book of James in the New Testament of the Bible, so I said "James" and Mr. Buckner smiled. I was so glad he smiled. Some students had never heard of James, the book, so they looked confused. Mr. Buckner explained, "Very good, Andy. When did you read James, which is your favorite book and which is a book that has been around for a long time?" I was so glad that Mr. Buckner knew about James. "I read it two years ago when I went to Vacation Bible School where I used to live." Then a student named Jennifer raised her hand and was called on. "I did that, too. I went to Vacation Bible School." So I sort of felt more at home because Mr. Buckner asked me if I would like to write a book about my new home. I told him I did not know much about this new home because I just moved here. Jennifer said she would help, so we used the newspaper and the computer and we made a really neat book about our city and it really helped me feel at home more. I liked Mr. Buckner's class best because we always read neat books and got to do really, really neat things. Plus, Mr. Buckner had some high school students come to our class to read with us. My high school reading buddy is Jeremy. He's a senior in high school and he is so smart.

⚜

Hi, I'm Jeremy Brannon. I'm a senior in high school. High school has been very tough for me. When I was in ninth grade I got in the LEARN program, which stands for Labor for Extra Academic Results Now. The program honestly tells you that lots of labor, very demanding work, will be required and that the results will be an extra challenging and extra worthwhile academic experience. Getting into LEARN was not completely my idea. My older brother was in LEARN and so was my older sister. They are smarter than I am, but I'm known for working hard. I do a lot around our house and during most summers I work on my grandfather's farm, so I know all about labor. The best part of LEARN was that every class included building things, making things, creating something, and actually seeing the results of your labor.

In U.S. government class we organized a presidential nominating convention and then a presidential inauguration. We built the stage, the signs, and we even used the school's television equipment to broadcast the events. In physics class we built all kinds of simple machines and systems with pulleys and levers and circuits. In English classes we used the school's auditorium and stage to produce our own plays and documentaries. We had to design the set and build it. In physical education class we built a set of golf clubs. It was not all that hard, but it sure taught you about the science in sporting equipment. Another option was to learn to restring a tennis racket. You can make some serious money doing that. What else, oh yeah, in geometry class we put the lines down on our school's new soccer field. Distances and angles never were so important as they were when we lined that field. You could really see and feel the equations and the theorems.

So, the labor part was matched with pretty interesting analysis, discussion, research, reading, and papers to write. The labor kind of got us interested and then the analysis or writing made more sense because we had actually done what we were analyzing and writing about and reading about. It would be really cool if school was like that all the time for everybody. I know my friends and I work harder at something we're interested in. It helps us realize why the work is worth doing.

It's like my friend who became an Eagle Scout last year. He worked so hard on that. I asked him why he did all the work. He had to miss some good times to go to scouting events. He said that it was always his goal to become an Eagle Scout just like his brother had been. His brother helped him some. But he told me that he had lots of choices about activities to earn each higher rank. He got to pick things he was interested in. He said that camping out on some mountain climb or cave exploration was so much fun. It was work, but it was fun because it was real life. He had to study and read and practice, but most of what he learned about camping came from actually camping out.

So, I think the LEARN program has me ready for anything I decide to do. I know I'll do well in college because, like my teachers said so many times, LEARN taught me how to learn, but also taught me to want to learn.

What are the classroom conditions in which extreme students thrive? What classroom atmosphere or environment can support the creation, nurturing, challenging, motivation, and academic success of extreme students? What can be done in classrooms to motivate students who have little or no commitment to school to become extreme students? What classroom actions can boost average students into the extreme student category? For students who are already extreme students, what classroom activities and classroom environment can fully challenge them, guide them, fascinate them, and fulfill them? The research presented in chapter 3 included seven characteristics of extreme students. Our topic now becomes what actions can be taken in classrooms to create, nurture, develop, and inspire these seven characteristics to emerge and/or grow through students' school experiences.

1. Extreme students are curious in a healthy, lively, purposeful way. Extreme students thrive in school when their wholesome curiosities are connected with what they are learning. Students, extreme students currently or yet to be extreme students, may reduce their commitment to or effort at school if their wholesome curiosities are numbed or are not applied due to ordinary activities and redundant procedures. The words "curious" and "inquisitive" were mentioned often in the research.

How can a teacher remain true to the school's curriculum and still connect the wholesome curiosities of students with what those students need to know? The teacher must fully know the curriculum with precise awareness of every specific skill, every idea, every concept, and every bit of information that students are required to master. The teacher then would find out what the wholesome curiosities of the students are.

Identifying the wholesome curiosities of students can be done in many ways, all of which provide useful information, yet there is another very human result—the students realize that the teacher is listening to them, learning about them, reading about them, appreciating them, and taking an interest in them. The sincere process of learning about wholesome curiosities of students helps demonstrate that students are one of the wholesome interests of the teacher.

Ask the students directly what their wholesome curiosities are, but first explain what wholesome means. Wholesome could be described as legal, ethical, and moral. Wholesome could be called G-rated for general audiences. Wholesome could be what your grandparents would approve of—sometimes society has to go back two generations for a superior and honorable standard of decency. Wholesome has boundaries so the students need to know that the teacher—the adult who is in charge of the classroom, who is responsible for professional and ethical standards to be upheld in this classroom, and whose intent is to properly cause intended learning in this classroom—requires that everyone will stay within those boundaries.

Asking the students can be done via a paper and pencil survey. This individualizes the activity and gives the teacher a written record to use throughout the school year. Some discussion could also be productive, but involving everyone in that discussion is important. Quick answer questions with a fast response from everyone can work. "What is your favorite sport?" "What is your career ambition?" "Where would you like to travel?" "If you could have your choice of any person to meet, who would it be?"

Communicating with students' former teachers is another source of information. Those teachers can provide efficient revelations about curiosities, interests, personality, strengths, learning styles, and more. But beware: a student today is not the same person he or she was a year ago. The information from former teachers or from a student's cumulative folder of school records can be insightful, but it is limited to what was known or done at certain times in the past.

Communication with parents and guardians can be helpful in many ways. Most families appreciate the expression of concern for and interest in their child. This can help build a favorable connection between the family and the school. This can help in case a future phone call about a problem is necessary, since the teacher has already established some trust and rapport with the family. Of course, families may leave something out or may exaggerate something, but generally the input from parents and guardians can be helpful.

Other teachers at your school may know the students and that input is useful. Remember, please, students do change and their interactions can vary. The way one teacher evaluates and works with your student may differ from how you evaluate and work with the same student. Give each student a wide open opportunity to be an extreme student in your classroom. Use sources of information to enhance the extreme student process, never to limit that process or that potential. What a student has been should not permanently limit what a student can be or become.

Listening to students is another way to become aware of their curiosities and interests. Students talk openly and honestly with one another about their interests and curiosities. Imagine this Monday morning conversation as students enter a classroom.

"Hey, what did you do this weekend? I called you once and e-mailed you once, but I never heard back."

"My fault, man. I was gone all weekend. My girlfriend's church youth group had this amazing forty-eight-hour ski trip. They let me go. It was so cool. What did you do?"

"Not much. I had to work Friday night and Saturday afternoon. That restaurant is so busy on weekends. It was packed on Friday. I went to a great movie Saturday night. It was so cool. The weather was pretty good on Sunday afternoon so I ran a few miles. I want to be ready for track this spring. I read all of the homework pages for history. It was so boring, but I need to get that grade up if I want to take the test for my driver's license. 3.0 average or no test."

Certainly connections can be made between the curriculum and snow skiing, part-time jobs, restaurants, movies, running, and getting a driver's license. The teacher is in the classroom as the students discuss weekend activities, so listening to the conversations sufficiently to take note of the topics of interest is worthwhile and is efficient.

Students are not reluctant to discuss their curiosities and interests. Before school begins each day, between classes, at recess, during lunch, at school activities such as sporting events, after school, and whenever asked, students naturally talk about themselves, their curiosities, and their interests. A teacher who is eager to hear what students are saying, thinking, wondering, feeling, asking, understanding, or misunderstanding just needs to purposefully be where students are and listen closely.

In the city where I live there is a skateboard park. It is one of my favorite places to visit. I watch with intense interest as children and teenagers develop their skateboard and rollerblade skills. These extreme sports are difficult to master, but the participants work hard, fall, get up, and try again. They advise each other, they encourage each other, they have healthy competitions with each other, they check to see if people are okay when they fall, they take turns, they analyze successful attempts at various stunts, and they evaluate unsuccessful attempts at other maneuvers. Watching these children and teenagers, listening to them, studying them, talking with them, and learning from them builds the possibilities for creating fascinating classroom activities that connect curiosities and the curriculum. Could physics and math improve skateboarding skills? Imagine the possibilities of skateboard science and rollerblade math.

In our economy, consumers are frequently offered incentives to encourage them to purchase products. Car manufacturers offer rebates, low or zero financing costs, and packages of low or no-cost accessories. Consumer products such as toothpaste, food, and beverages are available at reduced prices if consumers redeem a coupon from a newspaper advertisement. Furniture stores have sales on any and every holiday. All of these deals are designed to gain the attention of consumers and to persuade them to make a purchase.

In classrooms the product is learning. Teachers need not offer rebates, coupons, or holiday sales incentives. Few classroom incentives are more powerful than to teach in terms of what students are already curious about and interested in. Extreme students have a wholesome intellectual curiosity for knowledge. Connecting to and with that curiosity energizes the learning process, personalizes the learning process, removes the "when am I ever going to need this?" complaint, removes the "this is boring" complaint, and helps cause learning. This resource is available to every teacher at no financial cost. There is a price in terms of listening, thinking, interacting, creatively designing lessons, and boldly breaking some old habits and rules; however, the return on that investment of time and work can be increased quantity of and increased quality of student achievement coupled with more meaningful and rewarding career experiences for the teacher. Everyone wins.

Identifying the wholesome curiosities or interests of students, intentionally making curriculum connections with those curiosities or interests and what students need to learn can help bridge the gap between what students do at school and what they do in their real lives outside of school. Students respond deeply to activities that are real. Students are already dedicated to parts of life that are real to them. Bringing that realness of life as a resource for learning at school is an insufficiently tapped fuel for learning.

2. Extreme students ask questions. They are encouraged to ask questions. Their questions are taken seriously. Their questions become part of the body of knowledge in the classroom. Their questions help establish a student and teacher partnership, a classroom learning community.

"Tomorrow we will have a guest speaker. Because several of you have expressed an interest in professional sports, I have arranged for a major league baseball player to visit us tomorrow." My statement immediately generated a question from several of the eighth graders: "Are you serious?" The students accepted my answer that I was quite serious and that, fortunately for us, a former student of mine who worked his way through years of minor league baseball up to the major leagues was home for part of the off-season and had agreed to spend time with our class. I further explained, "Here are some index cards; there is one for each person. Please think a few moments and then write on the card any questions you would like for our guest to answer." The students completed the task quickly. After class I read their questions with satisfaction and delight. Their curiosity about professional sports and their interests in various careers were combined with their knowledge of economics. By giving them time today to think about questions, I reaped several benefits: (1) they reflected on what they wanted to learn, (2) they revised their questions to make each one precise, (3) they looked forward eagerly to class tomorrow, and (4) our guest speaker now had his presentation outlined for him, which he prefers so each audience learns and hears what is most important to it.

The students were captivated by our guest speaker. He spoke with sincerity, eloquence, and conviction. He answered all of the prepared questions plus more questions that students asked aloud during the presentation. He complimented the students on their good questions. The students were stunned when he told them that during most of his minor league experience he made $1,000 per month for each of the five months in the season. Students who dreamed of an automatic multimillion-dollar professional sports contract were learning some economic reality by asking an important question.

One way to encourage students to ask meaningful questions is to practice asking questions. That is what my eighth graders did in the example above. They were given time to think, which meant they asked important questions stated clearly. They knew their questions would be a major part of the class, so they were directly and personally involved in their education. They knew their interests were taken seriously. In addition to our guest speaker using the questions, I also used the questions to make connections with economic vocabulary terms the students had mastered.

Give students experiences in the classroom that generate important questions. Using prepackaged, prefabricated, generic, ordinary, impersonal worksheets provided by suppliers who do not know your students will cause one question to be asked repeatedly: "What do they mean in this question? I don't get what they want me to do." Who are they? Why are you letting them control the activity in your classroom? Worksheets do not inspire meaningful questions that lead to significant learning. Worksheets inspire procedural questions about "what do they want me to do," which is of use only to finish and then forget about the worksheets.

Meaningful questions can be inspired through a fascinating, connected, real variety of teaching methods and activities. If students play the role of reporters at a presidential news conference and the teacher plays the role of the president, a lively and intellectual question-and-answer exchange can occur. Students in a science class could create questions to ask current scientists and get those questions answered via e-mail or interactive websites. Students could invite an English or literature doctoral student to class and ask questions about an author on whom the student is becoming an expert. Art students could make lists of "five questions I would like to ask Leonardo da Vinci" and then do the research to discover likely answers da Vinci might have given. Music students could select a currently popular musician, a musician from one or two generations ago, and a famous composer, such as Beethoven, and perform a discussion featuring those three musicians talking to each other, playing their own music, and evaluating the changes of or constants in music over time.

Give the students a topic, an idea, an activity that is worth asking questions about and the questions will come. The questions are followed by discussion, explanation, analysis, debate, answers, research, and learning. The question-and-answer interaction helps create a classroom learning community.

I do require that students follow this guideline: Not everything that comes into the brain should come out of the mouth. Questions, yes, but questions that are acceptable in polite company. Teaching manners while we teach math, social studies, science, language arts, and other subjects is important.

We get more of what we reward, so reward questions. A simple way to do this is to compliment the student. "Great question, Troy." "Excellent thinking, Brian." "Super idea, Julie." "That's like what Robert was asking yesterday. Great connection of one idea to another, Kim."

Some seventh graders I taught many years ago sought this reward—to do better than they did yesterday. There were many facts the students had to know about current events, government, politics, geography, and history. We created the four-minute drill. We took turns; one student, then the next student, and on through the class. Then we would start the sequence of students again. "How many U.S. senators are there per state?" "How many senators total?" Our first score was thirty-seven correct answers in four minutes. "Could we do that again, please?" Of course. The goal became one hundred correct answers. The goal was reached. Questions were edited such as "senators per state" and "senators total." The sequence of questions did not change, so students memorized the initial thirty or so answers, which meant those questions were answered with no time needed for the questions to be asked. Within a few days the scores were regularly over 150. The new goal became 200. When the class reached 217, their cheers were of pure joy. They had perfected their skills, they surpassed their goals, they encouraged one another, they learned, and they were eager to learn more. I listened to and responded to their questions about improvements in the four-minute drill. No doubt, a teacher could reverse the approach and seek questions from students. "Okay, list five questions you would ask the president of the United States if he visited our school." "List five questions for college admissions so you learn how to get accepted to the college of your choice."

One more suggestion about asking questions relates to students who are extreme in their thinking, but not extreme in the outgoing nature that includes frequent participation in classroom question-and-answer discussions. Talk to that student individually outside of class. Hear his or her ideas. Ask if it is okay to quote him or her in class. "I talked with Tasha yesterday and she had this great idea. She would like for everyone in class to write a question for people in our town who used to go to this school. It's a way for us to research the school's history and help celebrate the school's fiftieth birthday. Let's think how to best do that."

The methods of asking for, inspiring, encouraging, seeking, applying, and answering questions are many. Establishing a classroom atmosphere in which students know they are working in a "questions are welcome here" zone is one necessary aspect of building and applying the question-asking characteristic of extreme students. A brain that has a question is a brain in which thinking is occurring and learning is ready to occur. Giving the students with such brains the environment and the activities that support questioning is a wonderful gift to the students and also for the teacher.

3. Extreme students are active within their own minds. They think, they wonder, they explore, and they analyze. They are given classroom activities and assignments that exercise their eagerness to think, wonder, explore, and analyze. Plus, for students who are not yet extreme students, their teacher appeals to the inherent characteristic of children and teenagers to be active within their own minds, to think, wonder, question, and probe ideas.

Young children are very active within their own minds. From the endless "why" questions they ask to the limitless imagination adventures of play they create, the mind of a young child is especially active. It is reasonable to observe that young children by nature fit the research description of extreme students based on the initial three characteristics: curiosity, questions, and vibrant mental activity. For the elementary, middle, or high school student who is no longer curious, asking questions, or vibrantly mentally active, what caused the change? Further consideration leads to a different approach. For the student who is not curious in terms of classroom instruction at school but exemplifies that characteristic at recess, at dismissal, during lunch, at school clubs, at practices for school sports, in the neighborhood with friends who are starting a band, with leaders and members of a Boy Scout or Girl Scout group, with a church youth group, at a part-time job or with family members at home or when the family goes out, what releases the curiosity, questions, and mental activity in those circumstances and what restricts the curiosity, questions, and mental activity in classrooms?

A high school student might say, "Well, classes are, you know, classes. It's just school. You have to do it. All those other things are interesting. You care about them. They are real. School, well, it's pretty much forced on you so it's hard to get very excited about it."

A middle school student might say, "Playing basketball with my friends after school is fun. Playing basketball at school in gym class is cool. I like basketball. Why can't other classes be like that?" An elementary school student might say, "My friends and I have so much fun. Even my brother and I have fun on weekends. Then it's Monday and we have school again. It's okay, but weekends are more funner. Reading class is best when we get to pick a book we like."

What would you say? What causes people who as young children were curious, asked questions, and were vibrantly mentally active to not be that way in fourth grade science class, eighth grade algebra class, or eleventh grade United States history class? What can be done at school to revitalize the ability, inclination, and willingness of those same people to once again be curious, ask questions, and be vibrantly mentally active?

For now, emphasize the characteristic from the research which tells us that extreme students are active within their own minds. What classroom learning activities can best stimulate, provoke, justify, inspire, and sustain worthwhile mental activity that will help cause the intended learning and could help students and teachers achieve many more good results than the intended learning only? Those results range from learning with and from one another to building commitments with one another, from creating a classroom community to learning at profound levels.

As you continue thinking about those topics, consider this example. A middle school student and I had some conversations about politics and current events. He was especially interested in international events. I asked him if he had ever read the *Economist*, a British publication. He said no, but when I told him more about it and later showed him a copy, he was increasingly intrigued. On the first school day of January he came up to me and with a big smile and said, "I got that magazine. For Christmas I got a copy of the *Economist* and I got a subscription to it." To support his vibrant mental activity, all I had to do was make him aware of a new resource.

⁂

We interrupt this chapter to bring you an important reality check. Some students are defiant. Some students are relentlessly defiant. Some students disrupt classes repeatedly and intentionally. Some students already have police records and/or juvenile justice records. Some students are criminals. The statistics available to me indicate that about 5 percent of public school students in middle schools and high schools are in the above listed categories of serious and severe misbehavior or illegality. Those students can be educated, but first they must be controlled and rehabilitated. After their behavior is corrected and other related issues are resolved, they can be educated. The control and rehabilitation process often requires an alternative setting and programs. It is unreasonable to expect one school at one location with one staff of traditionally educated teachers and administrators to provide the full range of educational and behavioral services to the range of students from juvenile criminals to children and teenagers who are in the genius category.

People who need open heart surgery cannot have it performed by their general family physician. The surgery needs to be done by an expert cardiologist whose specialty is heart surgery. It would make no sense for that patient to complain to the family doctor, "But you helped me with that infection last year. Why can't you fix my heart too?" For the heart problems to be corrected the patient needs a heart specialist. "Well, at least let me go to the hospital that is closest to home" might be a request of the patient, but that might not be best for the patient. "Well, that hospital is convenient for you, but another hospital a few miles away has a specialized cardiac unit which is exactly what you need." Some medical doctors specialize. Some educational alternatives specialize for similar reasons—to give the precise service that is needed. One doctor cannot provide all medical services and one hospital may not be able to provide all medical services. The same is true for one teacher and one school.

Students are already active within their own minds. They might not be as mentally active about school subjects, homework, tests, textbooks, research projects, or spelling words, but they are active within their own minds. Think, please, of reasons why I am suggesting to you that students are already active within their own minds. What did you think of? Now, what do you expect is a major reason I have for my confidence that students are already active within their own minds? Right you are. Students have wholesome knowledge, talents, and interests about which they are very mentally active. Some students are fascinated with basketball, so they are mentally active about basketball. They read about basketball, calculate statistics about basketball, study basketball, practice basketball, pay attention to basketball games or news or discussions, care about basketball, and, as a result, learn much about basketball. For other students their fascination could range from computers to music, from fashion to roller coasters, from reading to video games, from animals to art, from outer space to swimming, from cars to carpentry, from starting a business to finishing a marathon, from bowling to food, from their family heritage to museums, from vacations to world peace. When classroom activities connect the wholesome knowledge, talents, and interests of students—the topics and commitments about which students are already active in their own minds—with what needs to be learned at school, the results can be unlimited. A student's perspective may be helpful.

> If you fascinate me, I will learn. You want me to learn, right? You want me to be an extreme student, right? You want me to be curious to ask questions, to be active within my own mind, to be organized—you know, I mean, you are asking for a lot. You want me to read, read, and read. You want me to pay attention and work hard. Okay, I'll do all of that, but there's something you have to do first. You have to fascinate me.

When you fascinate me I become curious.

When I become curious I ask questions.

When I ask questions I become active within my own mind.

When I am active within my own mind, I get organized because I have a reason to get organized.

When I get organized I make time to read, read, and read.

When I read, read, and read I pay attention to what I read and to what it connects with.

When I pay attention and make connections I learn, really learn.

When I learn you become fascinated with what I accomplished.

So, please fascinate me and then I'll fascinate you.

4. Extreme students are organized. They manage time, materials, priorities, their behavior, and their pursuit of important goals with mature skills. Students who are not extreme students yet can be shown how to gain these organizational skills. In all likelihood, extreme students who have mastered these organizational skills have learned these skills, practiced these skills, observed these skills in other people, and acquired the skills by following those examples, developed the skills by direct instruction, or mastered organization skills in one activity—the work to earn a merit badge in scouting, the effort to achieve a rank at a summer camp, the demands of helping plan and manage a family move from one house to another—and then applied the skills to school in particular and to learning activities in general.

Organizational skills can be taught. Students who do the homework but never can find it when the time comes to turn it in frustrate themselves, their families, and their teachers. Those students may benefit from using a different colored folder for each class or subject. One pocket in the folder is clearly marked "homework to turn in." A brightly colored, easily removed note is attached to the homework page indicating the due date/time and teacher the homework goes to. A parent or guardian can supervise the night before and morning of each school day to check and double-check the folders and the homework. Families and schools can easily cooperate on this with telephone homework hotlines or school/teacher websites and web pages that provide daily updates on homework schedules and work done in class daily.

There are parts of school where organizational skills are taught and then expected. Coaches explain the schedule for sports practices and expect it to be followed. "Be in the locker room by 3:45. Be dressed and on the gym floor by 3:50. Complete stretching and warm-up by 3:55. Go to your drill and practice station for the day at 3:55. The list of stations and who goes to which station is posted daily in the locker room." Marching band directors, theater or drama presentation directors, orchestra or chorus directors, academic team coaches, and school newspaper sponsors could have similar schedules that are taught and students are then expected to discipline themselves sufficiently to follow.

Consider the organizational skills that can be learned through planning and completing a science project, a research paper, or other long-term assignment. There are many organizational steps, thinking steps, and learning steps in the science project. From identifying a topic to designing the structure of the experiment, from conducting the background research to following the sequence of the scientific process, from analyzing all results to making the report and the display of all findings, from presenting the findings to reflecting about what was learned about science and organization, this project can help students practice, apply, and master organizational skills.

Put a cell phone, a laptop computer, a DVD player, or other electronic innovation in the hands of a middle school or high school student and watch the application of some organizational skills. That same person may claim that he or she can never find their homework but can easily find any human being on planet earth by phone, text message, e-mail, or instant messaging. As with other characteristics of being an extreme student, it is altogether possible that an extreme student skill has been mastered in another part of a child's or teenager's life, it is just not being applied yet at school. Classroom activities that are designed to make the connection between skill use outside of school and using the same skill at school can be helpful. An activity in which students use carefully selected websites and e-mail addresses to research career interests and to ask questions of people in those careers is one example of transferring the Internet skills and related organization skills from social use to school use.

Classroom activities smaller in scope or shorter in time required than science projects or research papers can be effective in practicing, mastering, and applying organizational skills. When a class is going to read a novel, the teacher and the students can work together to establish the schedule for the weeks involved to read, study, analyze, and evaluate the novel. What pages are to be read by which day? What written work is due on which day? When will students create illustrations to demonstrate their understanding of the novel? What new vocabulary terms need to be known to fully comprehend the book and what activities will be done when, to master the vocabulary?

The daily sequence in a class can help students master some organizational skills. Knowing that class begins with the daily thought starter being copied from the board onto the next line in the notebook or folder for this class is a good beginning. Having the class agenda of activities on the board and indicating completion of each activity shows one approach to time management. Making every minute in class count exemplifies a strong organizational skill. "Great, we have three minutes left. Just enough time for us to practice the vocabulary terms for this week." For instructional productivity and teaching organizational skills by example, using a three-minute vocabulary drill and practice task is far superior to a default position, "Well, we just have three minutes left, so get everything packed up and you may talk quietly."

Have you known students who lost homework, did not bring materials to class, forgot a project was due, and had a locker filled with junk so that what was needed could not be found? Have you heard those same students talk about their collection of baseball or other trading/game cards and how precisely organized those cards are? Have you watched those same students participate in an organized sporting event that required bringing and/or properly using certain supplies? Perhaps some of those students are music fans and have large collections of songs organized on a computer or have a CD collection arranged orderly in a case. Some of those students might have a responsibility at home, at their church, in a family business, with a neighbor, for a grandparent, or for a friend in which they use and follow an organized set of procedures and plans.

The opportunity then becomes one of identifying with the student what he or she is already well organized with and showing the student how to apply the same skills at school. That skill transfer may not automatically happen with just a verbal, conceptual explanation. "Come on. You helped organize that Boy Scout toy drive for children at Christmas. Certainly you can organize your study schedule and homework." The desired behavior may have to be taught very directly. "You told me about that Boy Scout toy drive you helped organize at Christmas. Let's list everything that had to be done to plan that big project, to organize it, and to make it happen. Then we can take those actions you are already good at with Boy Scouts and figure out how you can use the same skills at school." It may also be useful for a superorganized student to show an unorganized student how organization is done. Communication from student to student sometimes has a precision and an impact that adult-to-student communication misses.

Of course, there are times when immediate action is needed. A locker that is full of missing library books, wadded up papers from months ago, a lunch that was not eaten last week, three jackets that were worn on three separate cool mornings and left at school when those cool mornings changed into warm afternoons, school books that are placed at gravity-defying angles, and a book bag that is crammed into the locker creating a bulge in the closed locker door that suggests imminent eruption, well that locker's contents may need to be completely emptied out on the floor now, and with an adult's help, the student throws away the trash, organizes books as if the bottom of the locker were a bookshelf, hangs up the book bag and the jackets, and discards the old lunch. The jackets are taken home today. The library books are returned now. The adult checks the locker with the student in a few days to be sure that another new mess is not replacing the old mess.

Organizational skills can be taught. Mastering organizational skills can help extreme students more efficiently and more directly apply their time and effort to thinking, learning, and achieving instead of wondering where they left a book or searching desperately for missing homework that may not have been done at all. Organization need not become a perfectionist obsession; rather, mastery of and use of the fundamental skills of time management, resource management, document management, and personal responsibilities can be sufficient to enhance the higher priorities of thinking, learning, and achieving.

5. *Extreme students read, read, and read.*

Despite the electronic revolution of the past century that brought innovations ranging from radios to computers, from record players to CD players, from movies to televisions, from cell phones to the Internet, people of all ages still read printed books held in the hands of the reader. Words can be listened to on tape, CD, the radio, and Internet connections. Text can be read on the computer screen or on the cell phone text messaging screen. Still, people continue a centuries-old process of opening a printed book, turning to the current page, and reading.

Why has reading a printed book endured through the ages in general and through the electronic revolution in particular? Book and reader have a unique interaction. Screen and reader miss some of the harmonious or argumentative interaction which is unique to book and reader. Readers respond to, think about, reflect on, react to, and interact with words in print differently than they do with words on a screen. Test that conclusion with this use of your imagination: if you received a written letter though the mail, sat down, opened the envelope, unfolded the letter, read the letter, reread the letter, and then thought about the content of the letter, how would that communication experience be different than if you received the same words, sentences, paragraphs via e-mail, instant messaging, or cell phone text message?

Perhaps the brain interacts with the printed word differently than it does with the electronic word. Perhaps the printed word interacts with heart, soul, and body more than the electronic word does. Please note, much that is useful, important, interesting, intriguing, and fascinating can be read via electronic transmission. Electronic transmission of text adds multiple sources of and delivery systems for reading materials. Extreme students read, read, and read from many sources, including electronic text; however, the research findings for this book strongly encourage those who would master the characteristics of extreme students to read books, printed books, challenging books, vocabulary building books, information building books, creativity inspiring books, idea stimulating books that the reader holds in his or her hands, closes occasionally to think about, opens again to write an idea on the border of a page next to an especially potent paragraph, reads further, and then returns to that powerful paragraph to reread, rethink, and learn anew.

"The book was better than the movie" is a common conclusion reached by people who read any book that was the basis for a movie. The book was good and the movie was good, so why was the book better? One reason could be the brain's interaction with ideas in print and the role of imagination, reflection, and pausing to think or reread. Movies in theaters are watched from start to finish with a different thought process that does not include much use of imagination because the picture on the screen defined the exact look of people or a setting whereas the words on the page become mental pictures that vary with the interpretation and imagination of each reader. Extreme students can learn in many ways through use of various methods, activities, and resources; however, the research for this book emphasized that abundant, vigorous, challenging, informative, frequent reading is an essential characteristic of extreme students.

What can be done in classrooms to create an atmosphere that supports, encourages, and successfully requires reading? What can be done in classrooms that results in a self-starting attitude about reading so students willingly and eagerly read, read more, and keep reading as they learn, comprehend, think, analyze, reason, create, imagine, and discover through reading. Perhaps an earlier idea can apply. If the goal is to develop the listening skills of students or the paying attention skills of students, then be sure that students are presented with ideas and activities that are worth listening to. How is this done? People pay attention to that which is fascinating, important, real, meaningful, useful now and/or creative, lively, and energetic. A logical extension of this reasoning indicates that people will read that which is fascinating, important, real, meaningful, useful now and/or creative, lively, energetic, and interactive.

The power of choice can also apply to reading. There are many times when each student must read the same material. How this reading material is presented to students, how its content is connected to their lives, how vibrant and intriguing the discussion questions are, how creative and personal the teacher is in leading a discussion about the reading to show relevance to life experience or interests of students, how very little (perhaps not at all) the teacher uses the generic materials provided by the publisher of the reading material, and how much importance is given to student input as a critique of the reading are some of the ways that required reading material can be made more fascinating to all students.

Still, when students can be given a choice of what will be read the power of choice—I selected this because it is of interest to me, because it has meaning to me, because my friend really liked it, because it looks really neat, because my favorite author wrote it, because my big sister said it is a cool book—can inspire more dedication to reading and can help create more productive reading.

Some teachers have discovered the unique impact of having students read material that their teacher wrote. A history teacher may use a paper he wrote in college as a resource for students to read. A science teacher could use an essay she wrote about her eighth grade science fair project as an introduction to scientific writing and to science projects. A language arts teacher's short story about teaching could help students learn all they need to know about short stories while also creating classroom interaction and insight that writing from authors the students do not know and who do not know the students would be unable to create.

Read, read more, keep reading can be inspired when a school takes one hour per week and everyone in the school participates in silent indoor reading. The students see the adults reading. The students selected books of interest. For this hour the school has the atmosphere of sustained intellectual effort that reading establishes. That atmosphere is protected from all interruptions or disruptions.

Inviting guests from the community, parents and guardians, grandparents, older students to read to students can inspire an interest in reading. Partnerships with local public libraries can help continue reading during the summer. Making school libraries available occasionally during the summer may have some logistical questions to answer, but could provide a valuable resource.

Extreme students read, read, and read. Through personal guidance from teachers extreme students realize that reading can be wholesome and productive, meaningful and rewarding, challenging and real, useful and inspiring. Extreme students read, read, and read, which helps students learn, learn, and learn while also giving students an important skill in learning how to learn.

6. Extreme students pay attention with total concentration.

Which is more fascinating—a basketball going through a hoop at one end of a basketball court during a basketball game or an idea going through a mind at the conclusion of a discussion in a classroom? Answers could range from "It depends on how close the basketball game was" to "It depends on what the idea was" to "Basketball, of course, because it's the most exciting sport" to "The idea, of course, because an idea can change a life."

If you visit a high school basketball game and watch the spectators, you will probably notice that most people are paying close attention to the game most of the time. Other people are socializing, standing at the concession stand, getting ready to leave and go home, talking with friends about something other than basketball, or paying partial attention to the game. If the game gets very, very close and one shot will determine the outcome, the crowd of spectators will probably increase its attention level. Even in basketball games the attention paid by fans can vary with the intensity of action on the basketball court.

Attention to ideas being explored in a classroom can vary also. When I promise students in economics class that they can acquire one million dollars, when I write $1,000,000 on the board, when they write $1,000,000 in their notes, the attention being paid is 100 percent. Knowing that 100 percent is possible in the category of paying attention, I set that goal as the minute-to-minute standard. As the students and I do the math of saving money for decades in an individual retirement account, they see how very possible it is to acquire $1,000,000 or more. They pay attention, think, participate, learn and the paying attention effort was made worthwhile.

I would suggest that the classroom has an advantage over the basketball court in terms of capturing attention. Some basketball games are especially thrilling as each pass, shot, foul, turnover, and time-out seem to have extraordinary urgency. The outcome of the game is in question until the final shot is taken just before the buzzer sounds to signal the end of the game. Other basketball games are 10-0 within three minutes and become lopsided blowouts, and some spectators leave at halftime. The most devoted basketball fans might watch every moment of any game with rapt attention, but for other fans the excitement level of the game determines the attention level paid by the spectator. Still other people have little or no interest in basketball and do not watch any games unless a relative or close friend is a participant.

Fans cannot control the action on the basketball court. Coaches cannot control the action on the basketball court. No one player can control all of the action on the basketball court. The most perfectly practiced set play can be discussed during a time-out, but when the game begins again and the players attempt to implement the designed play, it may not work as it was intended due to many human factors such as what the other team does to reduce the play's impact and what mistakes the team implementing the play make or avoid.

Teachers can design instructional activities that merit and earn the total attention of students. Basketball fans cannot go onto the basketball court and become participants in the game. Each student in each class can be a participant in every activity in the class. Reflect on the best teacher you have known. In that teacher's classroom students paid attention. In other classes the same students may have paid attention or not, but in this great teacher's classroom you are reflecting on, everyone paid attention. What caused that attention level to be high, consistent, and all-inclusive? It is very likely that the teacher did what great teachers do:

1. Used a variety of teaching methods and activities
2. Was enthusiastic about students and about teaching
3. Challenged the students
4. Made connections between what was being learned and the real lives of students

Those four characteristics of effective teaching can be used by all teachers in all classrooms. Using those four ideas is not a function of personality, so it is unacceptable to hide behind an excuse of "Well, I'm just not a very dynamic and energetic person. I'm not trained in theater or drama, so I can't put on a show. I'm just easygoing." Great teaching is not a function of personality types; rather, it is a result of doing what research shows and what your personal experience confirms that great teachers do.

Extreme students pay attention with total concentration. Some students always pay attention. Other students occasionally pay attention while still other students rarely pay attention. All students can and will pay attention with total concentration when what they are told to pay attention to is compelling, fascinating, meaningful, real, connected with their wholesome knowledge, talents, and interests. Even the students who require themselves to pay attention will more eagerly listen, participate, and learn when the classroom activities and atmosphere are brain food for their wholesome intellectual curiosity for knowledge.

Bless the hearts of the polite, compliant students who always pay attention, behave well, and cooperate no matter what the classroom activity or atmosphere may be; however, their good manners and compliant cooperation may not be matched by their maximum mental productivity unless the classroom activity and atmosphere are evoking that maximum mental productivity.

"Keen, this sounds great and all, but it seems so idealistic. At my school we have some very difficult students. It's hard to get anything done with defiant students, impossible to contact parents, bureaucratic regulations, paperwork, and meetings to attend."

Correct, and because of those realities it is mandatory that teachers do what works in the classroom. The trend in recent decades has been for local, state, and federal governments to require more of schools than ever. Societal trends further increase demands on schools and complexities of education. From more students being reared by grandparents to more students taking multiple prescription medications, there are unprecedented complexities facing schools today. Despite all of the difficulties imposed on schools, much worthwhile learning can still occur in classrooms. Students come into classrooms with wholesome knowledge, talents, and interests even if those same students come to school from a troubled family situation or with unusual medical conditions or other factors. Because teaching today is more complex, more complicated, more demanding, more exhausting, and more frustrating than ever and because the trends causing those realities will continue, it is absolutely essential for schools to do what works. We know what works. We know what great teaching includes and excludes. We know what causes learning, what inspires students, what fascinates students, and what challenges students. We know teachers who do all of that every day. We have been taught by some teachers who gave us magnificent learning experiences.

Imagine a teacher who has filed juvenile justice criminal charges against a few students. Imagine that same teacher being punched in the face by a student. Imagine that same teacher being verbally abused by a parent. Imagine that teacher realizing that those isolated events are not the parts that define the whole of a teaching career. Imagine that teacher working with group after group of students who excitedly think, listen, learn, offer ideas, complete homework, and succeed. Imagine that teacher working with class after class of students who make A or B grades and no grade below those successful levels. Imagine a teacher who was told by a sixth grader, "You're a great teacher." Imagine a teacher who views e-mailed pictures of a six-year-old child named for that teacher by two former students who began dating as they took that teacher's high school class years ago. That is my experience. Despite the occasional despair and heartbreak, there is much, much more achievement and joy. If we do our job correctly and completely, it is extremely hard, demanding, exhausting work. Yet it can touch our soul as we touch the minds and lives of students. Difficult? Yes. Worth it? Absolutely, positively yes.

If you are cut out for teaching, nothing else will do. If the calling on your life is to teach you must be where the students are. When teaching chose you and when you chose teaching it was with awareness that there would be some difficulties. But you were a person who could and would prevail because Tasha and Shawn need you and because you need Tasha and Shawn.

When school is interested in and interesting to Tasha, Tasha will be interested in school. When teachers are fascinated with and make learning fascinating to Shawn, Shawn will be fascinated with learning. When teachers and students experience classroom activities that cause extreme learning and are directed toward their mutual wholesome intellectual curiosities for knowledge, the dreams of every extreme teacher can come true and the potential for every extreme student can become real.

Observe students closely, listen to students intently, and talk to students with a sincere curiosity about their knowledge, talents, and interests. Find out what wholesome topics and activities have already captured the attention of students. Know about the parts of real life to which students are already paying total attention. Many students like cell phones. The science of cell phones could be the basis for some riveting classroom activities. Many students pay much attention to fashion. In terms of sociology, anthropology, economics, and technology, what can fashion reveal about people? A history lesson on the fashion of the 1920s or 1960s could be a way for students to understand those decades through a part of life that already captures their attention.

One way to create and nurture extreme students at school—children and teenagers who have a wholesome intellectual curiosity for knowledge—is to build on and connect with what those young people are already extreme students of in life outside of school. Why does math have to be textbook math or worksheet math? The goal is to learn math. One resource in reaching that goal is parts of life in which students are already using math purposefully, willingly, successfully, and accurately. When a teacher is truly frustrated with students who never pay attention in class, it can be important to discover what those students do pay attention to. Students have the skill of paying attention, but their attention is selective: "Fascinate me and I pay attention."

Perhaps it is no different than when teachers attend typical professional development programs and some teachers pay little or no attention despite knowing how to pay attention, knowing the importance of paying attention, knowing they are supposed to pay attention, and knowing that good manners require the courtesy of paying attention. The teachers are communicating, "Fascinate me. Make this real. Show me how this applies to me and I will pay attention with total concentration."

7. Extreme students work hard.

Hard work is good. The extreme student level is earned, is achieved, is reached through implementing the characteristics identified and explained in this chapter, plus one more that makes all of the characteristics go from idea to result: hard work. Hard work can be the difference between having a curiosity and fully exploring that curiosity. As a student goes from "I wonder why" to an extreme student's achievement of "I know why, I understand why, now with this new knowledge I have more skills than ever," a major reason for that transition happening is hard work.

Obtaining answers about the percentages of free throw shots made and missed until the correct answers are found requires hard, persistent, and sustained work. Practicing the spelling words for a test requires hard, persistent, and sustained work. Learning the new vocabulary in an international language class, designing and completing a science experiment, making sense out of a Shakespeare play, analyzing the Bill of Rights, mastering new computer software, writing and rewriting a paper about a novel, and preparing for a concert band performance all require hard work. Extreme students work hard.

What are the conditions, what is the atmosphere, and what is the environment in a classroom that inspires, justifies, encourages, applies, and rewards hard work? First, it is important to differentiate between hard work and busy work or being busy. The hard work that extreme students do and benefit from is productive, worthwhile, meaningful, useful, real, and fascinating. Going from two worksheets per class period to a new requirement of four worksheets per class period does not create the classroom experience of meaningful, purposeful, inspiring hard work. Second, hard work does not mean twenty-five hours' worth of tasks to complete in a twenty-four-hour day. The research for this book consistently endorsed work that was hard in terms of the depth required, the quality of effort involved, and the quality of the results obtained. Extreme students work hard in ways similar to how people work hard at a successful restaurant to provide superior service, superior food, and a superior atmosphere. Much attention to detail, precision, ingredients, quality, process, standards, and evaluation is exemplified by the restaurant management and is required of each worker.

At that restaurant, whether it be fast food or sophisticated formal dining, the hard work is apparent in the superior completion of the expected task. "They got our order exactly right, served us fast, and were so friendly even though they were superbusy" confirms the result of hard work. "That meal was perfect. It made our anniversary celebration a night to remember" confirms the result of hard work. Neither restaurant settled for good enough because great was possible, was required, and could be achieved through hard work.

Teachers who create, inspire, nurture, and encourage extreme students set a personal and professional example of hard work. "Today we solve the mystery. For centuries and centuries the questions have been asked. Today we will solve those mysteries of several millennia or, if you prefer, millenniums. We will probe the theories. We will explore the secrets. We will build our own model. We will search for clues. We will research existing knowledge. We will soon know, how did written language—words—begin. Before we travel in time, we travel electronically to the screen where I have projected an e-mail that was sent by one student in this classroom to me. Notice the use of words, abbreviations, symbols, and other unique e-mail or text messaging devices. Think for a moment—how did this electronic language begin?"

The impact of that introduction and the impact of that initial activity can be that students are intrigued, fascinated, thinking, and instantly convinced to work hard on today's learning adventure. The teacher has certainly worked hard to design, prepare, and implement this lesson. Her work is likely to be very efficient—students will pay attention, think, ask questions, be active in their own minds, organize their effort, willingly read, and eagerly work hard. She will probably not have to reteach the ideas and content being considered today because students will learn the first time. She will further build a classroom learning community as she and the students learn together, with and from each other. The students may never say, "Wow, Ms. Kelly really worked hard on our lesson for today," but they will respond to the teacher's hard work with their own hard work, which is a physical and mental way of confirming or saying, "Ms. Kelly worked hard on our lesson for today." Teachers who exemplify hard work—meaningful, purposeful, challenging, real, useful, fascinating, personal, interpersonal, and interactive work—are more likely to have students who respond by doing hard work.

"Keen, aren't there times when the work just has to be done? You know, it's just the nuts and bolts add, subtract, multiply, divide, memorize, read, fill in, turn in work that has to be done?" Yes, the work has to be done. The curriculum has to be mastered. The page has to be read. The math problem has to be solved. There can be far fewer times when the only reason left to give a student for doing work is "because it just has to be done, so do it now." Results can be enhanced if the reasons provided before "because it just has to be done" were included in a variety of teaching activities that convinced or inspired the student to do the work. As one high school student explained to me about his math class, "When teachers show me the why of each step in solving a math problem, I realize the need for each step and I do it. It helps show me the why." That very capable, conscientious, cooperative student will do the work required of him and more; however, he will work harder with the commitment that comes only through the power of a purpose when he knows the why of what he is being told to do. Knowing the why makes it worthwhile for him to do the work of an extreme student.

Here's an example. The homework assignment that follows was given to my eighth grade economics students. As usual, the assignment was given one week prior to the due date so everyone had ample time and so they could balance this assignment with other demands on their time. Every student turned in the homework on time and done well. I had checked with them individually and collectively in the days before the work was due to gauge their progress. They worked hard. They applied their curiosities. They were active and creative in their own minds. They organized their thoughts, time, and effort. They paid attention to the presentations in class. They experienced the characteristics of extreme students.

Create, invent, design, draw, and name a new product; write and present a television commercial for . . . a new and improved:

- Middle school classroom
- Middle school cafeteria

- Middle school back-pack/book bag
- Middle school library
- Section of middle school lockers showing details of one locker
- Middle school building
- Middle school gym
- School bus

On paper:

a. List at least 5 ways that your invention is different from its competition that exists now.
b. Tell how each of your 5 or more differences is better than what exists now.
c. Tell the name of the new item and why that is the perfect name for this new product/idea.
d. Show the new item via a drawing using at least 3 colors and using words (maybe like a map legend) to give details about the product, its features, how it works, what it does for the consumer. Think of this part as if it were a print ad.
e. Write the script and explain the setting/scenes of the television commercial—you will also present this commercial in class.

Bonus . . . makes a model/prototype of the new product.

We get more of what we reward. Students notice what is rewarded at school. Students notice what local newspapers report about schools. How many high school assemblies are held to reward and honor the achievements of athletes? How many assemblies in high schools are held to reward the academic successes of students? No doubt, athletes put much effort into their endeavors and they merit recognition, but that recognition should not surpass the celebrations for academic achievement. If educators say that learning is the top priority, but students see that touchdowns are rewarded more generously, more often, more visibly, more tangibly, and more publicly than academic achievement is rewarded, the message becomes contradictory or not convincing. "But learning should be its own reward." Then why isn't scoring a touchdown its own reward without a pep rally, parade, trophy, and more? When the school's academic team gets one paragraph in the newspaper on a little noticed page, but high school basketball scores are listed on the front page with detailed stories and multiple photographs in the sports section, what message is sent by the media? Educators can help increase the possibility of increased media reporting of academic achievements of innovative teaching activities and of human interest stories at school by calling, e-mailing, and meeting with reporters. Sending press releases and inviting reporters to school can also help. Not every press release will result in a news story about your school, but some reporters will eventually respond to a regular flow of news and ideas. In the next chapter we will confront some realistic and some imagined difficulties which could lead someone to doubt that the conditions which create, nurture, inspire, encourage, and fascinate extreme students can be implemented. First, we will join two extreme students for a day in their very real lives.

⚜

"Hey. How was that test in geometry?" Shawn could already tell that Tasha had no trouble with the test.

"Easy, easy, easy. Some proofs to do, but nothing to it. Finally geometry makes sense. I used to hate math, but, you know, this teacher is different. We used a cake recipe as an example of how to do a proof in geometry a few days ago."

"Are you serious? Sounds cool, but what's a cake got to do with geometry?"

"The cake will not bake right if you leave out one ingredient. Then we said that in doing proofs you can't leave out any facts or any steps. Made sense to me for the first time ever."

Shawn remembered something. "You know, my science teacher said we were going to do something with a big cake today. Something about layers of a cake and the layers of the earth. Anyway, let's hurry up and get to lunch before it's too crowded."

Tasha and Shawn found the typical crowded conditions of a high school cafeteria. Everyone sat pretty much in the same place with the same people every day. The only difference in the cafeteria today was the choices of dessert—Geometry Chocolate Cake, or Geology Layer Cake. The teachers must have worked this out with the cafeteria manager. Shawn and Tasha laughed as they took their desserts from the serving shelf to their trays.

"Hey, Tammy, what are you doing?" Tasha asked her friend who was standing at the end of the serving line.

"Oh, it's a project for statistics class. We're counting to see which cake people pick. We're counting the beverages people pick and how many people get pizza and nothing else. It beats going to class."

"Cool," Shawn replied. "I'd rather do math about cake and pizza than what we usually do."

"Yeah, me too," Tammy agreed. "Well, back to my work. See you guys later."

At the table Shawn and Tasha discussed the school dance that was coming up this Friday. Tasha said, "Did you hear about the band that is going to perform? No CDs or records or tapes this time. Actually two bands with students from this school will play at the dance. It all began in their music class. Some battle of the bands contest. The teacher set up brackets like in a tournament. Beethoven, the Beatles, jazz, country, and rap got matched up against each other and the final four was rap and country versus the two student bands. Neat idea, huh? The two student bands won and at the dance they both perform. Live music all night."

Shawn had heard something on the school's morning television news broadcast. "That is so cool. School dances never have bands anymore. I bet there's a huge crowd. What's it cost?"

"Not much," Tasha answered. The seniors in U.S. government class teamed up with the Salvation Army. It costs $5 per person or free if you donate three cans of food. The Salvation Army gets the food. My brother takes that government class. He said the idea was to show a way that citizens can help solve a problem without new taxes."

Their conversation continued throughout lunch. They discussed other plans for the weekend, homework due soon, what tests were coming up, who just got a new car, and a new movie theater complex that would open soon. As their lunch time ended, it was time to get to their next class. They both had ninth grade English next. When everyone sat down the teacher said, "Here's a list of all the ingredients that go into a homemade batch of cookies. Here's a list of the steps to take in baking cookies. Now, work together in your groups of five to create a two-minute presentation on "Baking the Perfect Cookie." The scoring guide we'll use to evaluate your presentation is on the board. Later I'll read a page from a cookbook about baking cookies. We'll see what is similar and what is different in the live presentation you make and the written presentation in the book. Any questions? Yes, Tasha."

"At lunch we had geometry chocolate cake or geology layer cake. The music class had their battle of the bands. Now our class is all about cookies. What's going on?"

"Wonderful question, Tasha. What's going on is curiosity and connections. Plus ideas and thinking. Then some excitement and learning. Some teachers traded ideas on different ways to teach and it really seems to work. Any other questions? No? Okay, please begin. We'll watch the first presentation in eight minutes."

❖

What were some teachers at Tasha and Shawn's school doing? They were creating, nurturing, intriguing, fascinating, and challenging current, emerging, or developing extreme students. Did those teachers need a change in national law or state law to permit them to teach this way? Did those teachers need changes in policies, regulations, or bureaucratic procedures? Did those teachers need permission for their classroom adventures? The answers are no, no, and no.

What did those teachers need? One good answer is that they needed an accurate memory that would remind them of the classroom experiences from their elementary school, middle school, and high school years that mattered most. That accurate memory would tell them about teachers who challenged them, inspired them, took an interest in them, made hard work worth doing because it connected to the real life of students, who were enthusiastic, who used a variety of teaching methods and activities, who listened, who were available for extra help, who liked students, whose classroom was orderly yet lively, whose students were polite and cordial, who gave students learning experiences that related to their interests, knowledge, and talent. When teachers reflect on and remember their best teachers, they are reminded that we know what works.

Did Tasha and Shawn's teachers use textbooks, handouts, overhead transparencies, drill and practice, tests, and homework? Yes. Did they use every other possible and available resource that would properly be used to cause learning? Yes. Did it work? Absolutely yes.

Despite those memories of great teachers and the confirmation that reflection gives to the research about what great teachers do, despite the research for this book about the characteristics of and the development of extreme students, some questions may arise. In the next chapter we explore those questions and their answers.

Chapter 5

But That Will Never Work

Yes it will. It already has. It is working now. You have seen it work. You have experienced it. The major issue is not, will it work, because it does work. The major issue is effective implementation so it works in more classrooms for more teachers and more students. First, let's directly deal with the persistent pessimistic pestering of the "that will never work" legion of doom and despair.

We go to a meeting of a high school's Curriculum and Instruction Committee. This group includes six teachers, one parent, and one guardian. The policy-making process for the school includes many committees with each teacher volunteering for or assigned to a committee. Parents and guardians are encouraged to join a committee. Each committee develops recommendations for the entire faculty and the parent organization to review. The school's management cabinet—principal, two assistant principals, one counselor, four teachers, and three parents/guardians—meets monthly to consider all committee recommendations.

The Curriculum and Instruction Committee has three topics on the agenda for the meeting: (1) the ninth grade failure rate, which shows an increasing percentage of ninth graders have failed at least one class for the year in each of the past three school years; (2) the student dropout rate, which has worsened in the past two years; and (3) concerns that students who are identified as gifted and talented are not getting classes, instructional activities, or other experiences that fully challenge and develop their abilities. The committee has been searching for solutions to these problems or concerns, and at this meeting the intention is to select a recommended action to help solve each of these high priority items. The committee participants are listed next. Please note, committee meetings are open to the public, and on this day one retired teacher, one local citizen who lives near the school, and two eleventh grade students attend the meeting.

Ms. Samuels: Thanks so much to everyone for attending our Curriculum and Instruction Committee meeting. I know that everyone is busy. We're starting right on time and we always promise ourselves to limit meetings to one hour. It's just hard to get much done after a long day is made longer with a meeting that goes on and on. So, let's get right to our agenda. Everyone has received the background reading. Thank you to Dr. Winston for gathering those articles from education journals to give us some perspective on our topics today. Our goal is to create recommendations for the management cabinet to consider as potential school policies. So, let's start with a summary of what we know about the first topic, which is the increasing number of ninth graders who fail at least one subject for the entire school year. For the benefit of our visitors I'll introduce everyone. I'm Ms. Samuels. I teach United States history and United States government. Mr. Maxwell teaches physics and astronomy. Mr. Lyon teaches chemistry. Ms. Nichols teaches freshman and sophomore English. Mr. Hernandez is our computer and technology teacher. Ms. Marshall teaches journalism and reading. Ms. James and Ms. Reynolds are parent and guardian members of the committee. Our visitors spoke to me before the meeting. Dr. Winston taught Spanish at this school for years until he retired. Mr. Jefferson owns several nearby businesses where some of our students work. Tricia Martin and Claire Todd are juniors at our school and they are covering this meeting for the school newspaper.

Let's start. Mr. Hernandez, you have prepared some ideas about the ninth grade failure rate. Please begin.

Mr. Hernandez: In one of my computer classes the students and I searched website and other online resources to get ideas and information about ninth grade students. We found many articles and studies about separate buildings for ninth graders, using one section of a building as the ninth grade wing, borrowing some middle school ideas and having ninth graders in groups of 150 students taught by a team of six teachers, a two- or three-day high school preparation camp in the summer to help the ninth graders make the adjustment from middle school to high school, all sorts of reward and incentive programs, parent involvement programs, after school and before school homework help sessions, mentor programs, small learning community programs so individual students do not feel lost and alone in a very large high school, and a school that brought back some classes such as the woodworking shop, home economics, sewing, and architectural drafting. I sent an e-mail survey to our faculty to get their input. I sent an automatic dial survey to all families in the school and I sent an online survey to every family we have an e-mail address for. We have much input on the ninth grade failure rate topic.

Dr. Winston: It's interesting to hear that this topic is being discussed again. Maybe ten years ago we had a ninth grade task force to study the same topic. That resulted in many changes. We went to block schedules so students did not change classes as often, but that did not impact the ninth grade failure rate. We brought back the old homeroom idea. We began character education for every ninth grader every day through homeroom. We gave free to every ninth grader a planner book so they could organize their homework and daily schedule. I think some of those changes are still used, but others faded away because the results were so limited. The ninth grade failure rate did not change much even with all of those efforts.

Mr. Hernandez: Many teachers mentioned those changes in their survey answers. One teacher said "here we go again. The same old programs will probably get the same old results."

Ms. Marshall: I've always thought that reading was essential. I teach reading to students who are two grade levels or more lower than their age-group in reading. My classes are mostly ninth graders because we need to get them up to grade level in reading as fast as possible. I know some people think my students don't work hard because they use a different curriculum and different books, but when a fourteen-year-old goes from seventh grade reading level to ninth or tenth grade reading level in one year it is a big deal. Maybe some of what we do in reading classes could work in other classes for ninth graders.

Mr. Maxwell: Were there any ideas that came from the online research and surveys you did, Mr. Hernandez?

Mr. Hernandez: Most of what we found were ideas that are similar to what this school has tried before. Some changes got one or two years of improved results, but then the progress stopped as the original interest in the change declined or as the people who supported the change moved to other jobs. A few schools were convinced that the homeroom idea could work, so they experimented with variations on it. A few schools converted daily homeroom into a weekly activity period. Each teacher sponsors an activity period club and every ninth grader is in a club they select. The topics ranged from cake decorating to website design. Ninth grade attendance on activity period day was always up. Ninth grade behavior on activity period day almost always showed few if any discipline referrals to the office. Maybe Tricia and Claire could tell us what they think students would say about an activity period.

Tricia Martin: We have so many clubs and sports at school, but, I guess, some students can't get involved because of jobs after school or family situations. I'm in some clubs and I play soccer. It's great. No offense, but the clubs and soccer are some of the best parts of school.

Claire Todd: Yeah, I play softball and I know how hard I work at it. If school did not have softball I'd be pretty bored. If ninth graders could be in a club they like, it might give them a reason to do better in school like softball does for me.

Ms. Nichols: That does make sense. I notice the same thing in my students. I really try to find interesting stories and books for us to read in ninth and tenth grade English. We use sports articles, newspaper stories, interviews students conduct, job applications, and other real information. The students groan when we have to use the huge literature book, but they get so interested when I bring in a newspaper or magazine story. Here's my conclusion—I can teach most of the English curriculum with some creative materials. Since the students get so interested in other reading materials, I use them more and more while I use the textbook less and less. I've noticed better grades from students on projects like these. They tell me it's because the newspaper stories are more interesting than some short story from a century ago. As long as they learn English that's fine with me.

Mr. Lyon: I think there is some chemistry at work here, which pleases me because it shows that my subject does apply to life outside of the laboratory. Tricia and Claire are in my honors chemistry class so I wanted to point this out especially for them. There was a chemistry with the activity period when students and teachers worked together on interests they shared. The same chemistry worked in English classes where interesting news articles were used to teach writing and language skills. There's a big idea in all of this that maybe could help with the ninth grade failure rate.

Ms. Samuels: Let's be careful here. School can't just be fun activity periods and easy to read newspaper stories about some basketball team. School has to include some serious work that has to be done whether people like it or not.

Ms. James: Maybe that's why some ninth graders fail. The work has to be done, but they can't see any reason to do it or any use for it. The only reason some students have for doing the work is they get in trouble if they don't do the work. I run a business from my home. The company I work for has sales representatives everywhere. We have sales contests, incentives, and bonuses all the time. Still, I work hard because I really believe in the products. I could find another company that would pay me as well as this company, but I really care about getting these health and nutrition products to people. I believe in my work. How many classes and homework assignments inspire that kind of commitment from students? Sure, I have to do accounting, paperwork, and e-mail reports for my job. That work has to be done, but I know it is part of the bigger work I really believe in. So, since I'm interested in the products I sell and the people I sell to, I work hard by choice. I know teachers work hard, but if every student saw and knew that teachers believe in the importance of what they teach it would be motivating. If students saw and knew that teachers deeply care about the students, that could be motivating too.

Ms. Reynolds: I know what you mean. My grandson is a sophomore. He barely got through ninth grade. There was this one teacher last year who heard Carlos talking about a car he works on. It's my husband's car, but Carlos is helping him fix it up. It's a car from the 1960s, but they got it to run and they made it look like new. Well, the ninth grade English teacher found some technical books about cars and creative stories about how cars influenced our society and our culture. So Carlos gets excited about reading. He makes an A on a test because he studied and paid attention and because on one test question he got to pick the topic to write a letter about. He wrote a letter to a car company president. Perfect spelling, perfect punctuation, and perfect format. So he began taking school more seriously. He did what Ms. James said. I think it was because one teacher showed Carlos that school and cars could go together.

Mr. Jefferson: Well, what's our conclusion? Mr. Hernandez, from your research and our discussion what's our recommendation? I have one idea. I see how hard students work at my businesses. Sure, they earn money, but there are other places to earn money. They work hard and they stay with my businesses year after year. Here's why—I talk to them, I listen to them, and I use their ideas. They tell me what new menu items to serve at my restaurants. They tell me about the right posters or pictures to put up. They designed my websites. They created some of the contests we have at my bowling alley. I think the best thing I do for them is take them seriously. Then they take their job seriously. It's good business. It's a good way to treat people. It's probably good for schools to do the same thing.

Mr. Hernandez: Our surveys and research found lots of training programs for teachers, lots of academic help programs for students, all kinds of school to home communication ideas or devices, but there was one overall conclusion that came from students, teachers, and families. They said how so many students just see high school as something to get through, to finish and get out of as fast as possible. Students who really liked high school mentioned clubs and sports much more than classes. Still, some students mentioned certain classes that were interesting, were the ones they learned the most from and worked hardest for.

Ms. Samuels: Okay, what do we recommend to the school management cabinet? That somehow we make everything at school as interesting to students as clubs are and as sports are?

Claire Todd: Please, please do that.

Ms. James: It's hard to argue with the idea that people work more when they are interested in what they are doing. How do we make every subject at school interesting for every ninth grader who might fail a class or two and become part of the ninth grade failure rate?

Ms. Samuels: That's logical. Now, in a high school of 1,950 students including almost 600 ninth graders, how is that done? I mean, how do you individualize anything for that many people?

Ms. Reynolds: Remember what I said about Carlos. His teacher knew how to do that. She individualized his reading. I think other students read about money or sports or outer space and different things. She made everyone learn the English, but it could be done in various ways. Ask her. It was, it was, Ms. Katie Brooks. She still teaches here. Ask her how to do that.

Ms. Samuels: In the interest of time, we need to finish this topic and move on. Let's have Ms. Brooks attend our next committee meeting. Between now and then, I'll talk to her and we'll see what records, lesson plans, or other materials she has. If it's okay with her, I'll observe a class to see how she is doing this. If someone at our school is already getting great results with ninth graders, let's tell other people about it. Maybe there are other teachers succeeding with other students like Carlos. We might have more examples of success here than we thought. Okay, Mr. Hernandez, can you send part 2 of a survey with an emphasis on what has worked, please. Let's identify our successes and show people what works right here. Thank you, Mr. Hernandez. Now, our next topic is the dropout rate. Is anyone thinking what I'm thinking? Is this discussion going to sound a lot like the ninth grade failure rate discussion?

Mr. Maxwell: Part of it may be similar, but there are some unique complexities with dropouts that are different from ninth grade failure rate. Failing a class or two in ninth grade is bad. Dropping out is horrible.

Mr. Lyon: You can find dissertations, books, studies, government-funded reports, and more about dropouts. You can check how different the laws are from state to state. But we all know that a student who failed a year in elementary school and then fails another year in middle school begins ninth grade at fifteen or sixteen years old. They won't stay here and graduate at age 20. Unless we give them some way to move faster and graduate at age 18 or 19, they will drop out. One student told me he could make $300 per week at a car wash and that was all he cared about. I asked him what he would do when machines washed the cars and his job was eliminated. He smiled and said it would never happen.

Ms. Nichols: Some people drop out because of family problems or they keep getting in trouble with the police or they get pregnant. Those are tough situations. When I became a teacher it was so I could teach, but some of our students need social workers or psychiatrists or probation officers more than they need a teacher. Then the other students who do cooperate and work hard don't get as much of our time as they deserve.

Ms. Marshall: The dropouts I have known had trouble with reading and that meant they got far behind. They never catch up so they quit.

Dr. Winston: This problem is an old one. There is no perfect solution because different students drop out for different reasons. I laugh at the Congress and other politicians when they give their lofty speeches about no dropouts, no failures, no child left behind. Let's see those same people come teach for one year. They'd never last that long. The speeches are easy to give. The work is hard to do. I think there was one idea years ago that did work. We had a new counselor and a new principal who came to this school at the same time. They had worked together somewhere else and their other school reduced the dropout rate. How? They never talked about the dropout rate. They talked about CHESS, which stood for challenging, helping, encouraging successful students. The ideal CHESS level was 100 percent, meaning no student failed a class for the school year, each student stayed on track and on schedule to graduate from high school in four years, and no student dropped out. Every teacher was given a shirt and a hat with the CHESS team logo on it. They got great results. The emphasis was staying in school to succeed instead of emphasizing not dropping out.

The most effective part of CHESS was that every teacher, administrator, counselor, plus a few retired teachers and some people who worked at central office in the school district had their own CHESS team of ten high school students. The adult and the students met once each week for a thirty-minute CHESS class. The class was everything from homework help to conflict resolution and people skills. The adult sent at least one encouraging e-mail to each of the ten students each week. The teachers increased the challenge of classes not to make them just work more, but to make them more connected with each other and with real life. Students were challenged to think of connections between various subjects and between school classes and their own interest. Teachers took turns arriving early so students had places to study each morning. The results were very good. Not 100 percent, but way ahead of where they began.

Ms. Samuels: What happened to the CHESS teams? We don't do that anymore.

Dr. Winston: The principal and the counselor moved on to new jobs. The program faded away.

Ms. James: Did you hear what Dr. Winston said? It's so much like what we said for the ninth grade failure rate, just like Ms. Samuels predicted. Why have a different solution for each problem if one solution can help solve lots of problems.

Mr. Jefferson: Let's be sure we understand what that one solution is.

Tricia Martin: I think I figured it out. I know I'm a student and you are adults, but I really think this makes sense. Claire and I were just writing each other a note. What we said is what Ms. James may have been thinking. I mean, it's all so obvious when you think about it. Claire, you tell them. It's what you just wrote.

Claire Todd: Okay, it's like, we work harder on stuff that interests us. You know, stuff we care about. And we work harder for people who like us and care about us.

Ms. Nichols: Claire, that makes sense. I know it is true. I just know that some parts of schoolwork have to be done whether it's interesting or not and you have to work for teachers no matter how well you get along with them.

Mr. Jefferson: Yeah, the work has to be done and the adults have to be obeyed, but what Claire is saying is exactly why the students who work so hard at my businesses actually work hard willingly. They are interested in the business because their ideas and suggestions get used. That means the business is partly their creation. They want it to succeed because it reflects on them. They work hard for me because they know I like them and they know that I work for them. That's why I'm at this meeting.

Ms. Samuels: So, how do we get Mr. Jefferson's system from his businesses to work at school so fewer students drop out?

Dr. Winston: We have to be realistic. One reason Mr. Jefferson's system at his stores works is because he pays the students who are his employees. Of course they will work hard for money. We can't pay them at school. Every now and then education tries to borrow ideas from big corporations or other businesses, but they don't always work. A business owner can fire an employee. We can't fire students. And remember what caused the CHESS plan to fade away. The people who started it moved away to other jobs. It will take some very determined leadership to get anything done to reduce the dropout rate or the ninth grade failure rate.

Ms. James: I keep thinking of the company I work with. Sure, it's a business and not a school so there are many differences, but using their thinking might give us some ideas. The married couple who started the company uses this slogan with all of the employees: "Don't sell products. Solve problems." I don't sell health and nutrition products. I help solve health and nutrition problems people have. My job is to help people feel healthier and be healthier. My sales presentation is a lot of questions I ask and a lot of listening to the answers people give. Then I suggest products that could help solve the problems they told me about. Isn't that an approach we could take at school? Can't we present school and classes and subjects and clubs or sports as solutions to problems or as great opportunities that you don't want to miss?

Ms. Samuels: So, where are we on the dropout problem? Is there any clear idea emerging?

Mr. Lyon: I'm the chemistry teacher so let me add that perspective. First, I've seen several changes in how we teach chemistry through my career. Use the textbook changes to don't use a textbook. Use experiments all the time to use experiments occasionally but spend more time having students analyze, think about, and write about the experiments. Use videos and the Internet, to use more class discussions. So, we change for a few years and then change again and then change a few years after that. It's frustrating because it wastes so much effort and money. I've never seen any of those changes produce very impressive results, but we'll probably be told soon by the state or the school board or the management cabinet to change again. Then a new governor or a new school district superintendent or a new principal will come in and change it all again. Well, as a chemist I can tell you that is bad science. We evaluate scientific experiments to see what happened and why. Some of these changes in schools over the years had little fancy evidence to support them, so we just follow one fad or we just watch decisions made to satisfy some loud interest group that complained to the governor or to the school board.

Mr. Maxwell: You know, in physics and other sciences there's been some work in recent years on different theories about how substances, particles, materials, elements, and chemicals interact under varying conditions. Complexity theory and chaos theory offer ideas. Nanotechnology is another emerging field of thought and discovery. I sometimes think of each class of twenty-five or thirty students in terms of these theories. How do the students react to me, to each other, to physics? I analyze what works and what does not work. I try to minimize the disruptions Mr. Lyon mentioned that all the "here today, gone tomorrow" changes in education bring. I just teach physics. I usually begin with a bicycle and a skateboard and a pair of old-fashioned roller skates plus a pair of new rollerblades. The students know these things and have used them. We explore the physics in each item and just go from there to more everyday applications. I don't think about failure rates or dropout rates. I think about physics and students and how to be sure everybody learns everything. It seems to work.

Ms. Samuels: Maybe Ms. Brooks and Mr. Lyon are on the same track. Maybe some of the ideas and answers we need are right here at our school.

Ms. Marshall: You could be right. We keep bringing in all of these speakers to our school district or our school. They get paid a lot of money to tell us what to do and then they leave town to get paid a lot of money in another city to tell other people to do the same thing they told us to do. How does that help us? Our school is unique. Some guest speaker from who knows where is not an expert on our school or our students. What's wrong with asking our teachers and our students what is working here and then showing everyone how they can use what is already working?

Ms. Samuels: Good idea. Let's be sure we ask for very specific actions. If a teacher says that what works is she gets to know her students, we need to know how she gets to know them. If a student says he does well in one class and does poorly in other classes, let's find out what is working in that one class and try to duplicate the reasons for the success.

Mr. Hernandez: That survey is easy to do. I can e-mail it to teachers tomorrow. Well, I'll send a rough draft to all of you tomorrow and make changes that you suggest, so reply to me fast and I'll send the revised survey in a few days. We need to ask students for their ideas. Maybe our school newspaper's online version could do that. How about a special issue?

Claire Todd: We've done special issues before, so that should be easy to do. If Mr. Hernandez can work with us on how to write the survey, we can do that really fast.

Ms. Nichols: So we're asking teachers and students to tell us what works, right? What gets good results in classes? What gets students to make good grades and not flunk, right? That seems so simple. It's not some big proclamation by the president, it's just basic common sense to do what works best. Good plan.

Ms. Samuels: We need to get to our final topic for this meeting. Our school has several hundred students who have been officially identified as gifted and talented. The truth is that we don't do enough for these students. It is wrong to say that they are smart so they'll be fine on their own. They can't learn about something they have never heard of. They can't learn completely if they are taught in the same way every day, every year. They can't develop their gift or talent without intense challenge and direct guidance. So, how do we provide the best possible education for our gifted and talented students?

Ms. Marshall: There is good news on this. There are national and state organizations exclusively dedicated to gifted and talented education. If there is any part of education that has answers to questions, success stories, books, and examples of what works, this is it. I went to a state level gifted and talented education conference for two days last summer. There was one fancy guest speaker from far away who spoke for two hours. I got one good idea from that speech. Then the rest of the time was spent going to presentations by teachers who taught lessons they had actually used with gifted and talented students in mind. I got dozens of great ideas. Some of the teaching methods for gifted and talented students can work with many students, maybe all students. I'm using the ideas from that conference and I'm making changes based on what I know about my students. The results are really good. You know, what I learned at that conference and what I'm doing new in my classroom is going to be my answer to the survey Mr. Hernandez sends us. I think some other teachers at this school have gone to conferences like the one I attended. Let's get their ideas. Maybe the survey could include a question so teachers can tell us what they are doing for gifted and talented students that works really well.

Ms. Reynolds: It's so amazing to listen to the ideas from this meeting. We are getting really confident that people at this school already have solutions to problems at this school.

Dr. Winston: Be careful with that optimism. People will always complain. People resist change. People will say that an idea will never work here. But if you find the ideas that are already working here, that outsmarts one complaint.

Ms. Samuels: Our time is almost out. Mr. Hernandez will send all of us a rough draft of the survey. He will revise it and send it to faculty and staff in two or three days. Claire will work with Mr. Hernandez for the student version of a survey. I'll work with Mr. Hernandez and Claire to compile the survey results. We'll ask some of you to help with that. Then we'll meet again in two weeks to review the ideas from the surveys so we can make our recommendations to be school management cabinet. Our principal encourages committees to get lots of input, but I'll e-mail him right now so he is aware of the new surveys. Thanks to everyone for your time and work today.

Think, please, of some observations and some conclusions you can make based on the committee discussion presented above:

1.
2.
3.
4.

Perhaps your observations and conclusions included some of these thoughts or perhaps your ideas are different, so let's compare and contrast our reactions to the committee's discussion:

1. Effective implementation of good ideas will get favorable results.
2. Every school has successful students and teachers. Identify what is causing those successes, tell other people about those successes, and show other people how to implement the ideas or actions associated with those successes.
3. Students who fail one or more classes may be doing acceptable work in another class. Identify what is causing that other class to go better for the student and apply those findings in every possible way.

4. Committees and bureaucracies, laws and policies do not truly reform education. Individual people doing outstanding work reform education in the ultimate way—favorably impacting what and how a student learns.

5. Committees, bureaucracies, laws, and policies can play supportive roles in improving education. Those roles are enhanced if decisions and actions of policy-making, regulation-making, law-making, budget-making, and decision-making officials follow two guidelines: (1) The Tasha and Shawn rule. Ask yourself, how will this action or this decision improve education for Tasha and Shawn, who are real students? (2) If I were a teacher being impacted by this action or decision, would it help me do my job or make it harder for me to do my job?

6. Rather than creating one or more separate programs or initiatives for each problem at school—the ninth grade failure rate program, the dropout prevention initiative, the gifted and talented reform—take the collection of high priority problems at school and, whenever possible, search for the one or two comprehensive actions that can do the most good for the most people to help solve the collection of problems.

The committee discussion was orderly, cordial, productive, optimistic, and action-oriented. As word of the committee's thinking, planning, and upcoming actions are communicated some reactions will be supportive, some reactions will be neutral, some reactions will be apathetic, and some reactions will be belligerent. Consider the following discussion of two teachers during their early morning duty supervision in the school's front hall.

Mr. Knox: There they go again. None of that will ever work. Can you believe all of that feel-good happy talk from the Curriculum and Instruction Committee? We've done all of that before. It's a waste of time. What are they thinking?

Ms. Serviss: When did you become so cynical? What do you mean by feel-good happy talk? I read the e-mail minutes of the committee meeting. They were working on important topics and seemed to be very practical. I'd say it's very realistic to ask our own people for their best ideas. It's sure better than another major overhaul of school dictated by somebody else. I'd rather do this ourselves than have people who don't work at our school tell us what to do.

Mr. Knox: Come on, that's not my point. Ninth graders fail because they are lazy and don't work. I've taught ninth grade and it was the same thing every year. Some students did well, others did average, and others flunked. I've seen every program that ever existed. I've seen early morning homework help, peer tutoring, homework hotline by phone, homework website information and help, after school tutoring, new classes and subjects that were easier to pass, culturally sensitive education, senior student and freshman student mentor teams, community volunteers to mentor students, reading incentive programs, work-study programs, second chance to pass programs, and federal government programs. Get my point? I've seen it all. Nothing changes. Good students succeed. Average students get by. Failing students keep failing and quit. How can we change something that is just part of reality? It's the real world. Not everyone does great in life. School is no different.

Ms. Serviss: What radio talk show have you been listening to? Those ultraconservative radio hosts and callers who beat up the schools day after day must send you a transcript of their programs. You've memorized your speech and you almost sound like you believe it. You've seen students improve. It's our job to keep looking for ways to teach every student.

Mr. Knox: My job is to give every student a chance to learn. I can't study for them. If they have a chapter in the textbook to read it's their job to read it. Why should we have to pay for early morning homework help supervision or after school tutoring or some expensive summer program to get students caught up? I've been doing this long enough to know the realities.

Ms. Serviss: You've been here longer than I have, but I've taught at this high school and at one other high school. I've known students who were going nowhere as freshmen get turned around and graduate on time. Those students almost always said that a teacher who took an interest in them and just refused to let them fail made the difference. So that sort of agrees with you and with the committee. Maybe we don't need program after program and change after change. We just need to do what works like one teacher making sure that one student knows that someone is on their side and will do whatever it takes to get them through school.

Mr. Knox: That almost made sense. We certainly do not need any more new programs at school. Let's just teach. Every new government program or community program just creates more meetings to attend and more paperwork to do. But, if a teacher does everything possible to help a student, the student still has to do the work, the reading, the studying, the homework, and all the rest that makes them succeed.

Ms. Serviss: I understand that. The committee is asking everyone to tell what they have done that got those results. In this school every day lots of good work gets done by teachers and students, but we only know what happens in our own classrooms. Doesn't it make sense to trade good ideas?

Mr. Knox: Maybe so, but the best idea of all is for teachers to be left alone to teach. Eliminate the interruptions or meetings or paperwork. And the other good idea is for students to take school seriously and do their work.

Ms. Serviss: Maybe the committee will be told of ways to make that happen. There's the bell. Time for class. Have a wonderful day, Mr. Knox. Show those students how to learn.

Mr. Knox: Right. They know how to learn about driving cars or playing soccer. If I could only get them to work on math the way they work on their cars and their sports.

Does Mr. Knox realize how important his last statement is? The same students he is convinced will not work at school no matter what anyone does are already very eagerly working on learning to drive a car so they can get their driver's license. They are already working hard at soccer, other sports, clubs, other wholesome interests. These students are learning about and are working on cars or soccer, which confirms that they are able to learn and to work. As the high school student told me, "Show me the why of each step in a math problem so I know the reason to do it." Students know the why of learning to drive a car or learning to kick a soccer ball with new expertise. The why of some or all of school may not be known or may not be convincing. "Because it will be on the test this Friday" is not the most convincing or motivating reason to know something. "Because this connects with your favorite hobby and your career goals. I'll show you how this math connects with driving a car and with owning a car dealership." The power of why, the power of connections, the power of teachers doing what great teachers do can add up to the absolutely certain power to create, nurture, encourage, challenge, and develop extreme students.

Yes, education faces a mountain of problems. There are school buildings that needed significant repair decades ago. Students use some technology systems that are several updates behind cutting-edge machines, capabilities, and ideas. Students who are convicted criminals are allowed to be in school despite a career of crime that clearly says they need to be educated elsewhere. The federal government is increasing its role in education despite no evidence that Washington, D.C., can effectively micromanage schools. Students and teachers are concerned for their own safety at some schools, but investments in school law enforcement officers, surveillance cameras, and metal detectors have not kept pace with the reality of safety concerns. Every new societal problem from more children being overweight to more children not speaking English becomes another duty for schools to accept and another problem for schools to solve. These issues and others merit serious, sober, practical, and accurate review with sensible actions taken as needed by schools and/or by other groups and organizations; however, the growing number of societal issues imposed on schools need not create excessive complications such that schools become social service agencies instead of schools. Just because schools are buildings where children and teenagers come about half of the days in each calendar year does not mean that every societal issue, initiative, or program directed toward children or teenagers should be implemented within schools. The purpose of a school is to cause learning. Keeping true to that purpose can help filter out actions or complications that do not help cause learning.

The Curriculum and Instruction Committee has dedicated itself to identifying what is causing learning in their classrooms and with their students. That makes sense. Despite the bureaucratic difficulties, no matter how well intentioned, that the president, the U.S. Congress, state officials, local officials, or community activists create for schools, when people at a school identify what is working for teachers and students at that school and then do much, much more of what works so the entire school becomes a "we do what works school," the results can be very beneficial.

For a few minutes, think about school as a student does. What impacts students at school more than anything else, more than anyone else? What impacts the experiences students have at school moment to moment, day to day more than anything else, more than anyone else? Let's ask Tasha and Shawn.

Tasha: My friends are the best part of school. Seeing them every day and just talking to each other about stuff. Making plans for the weekend or for after school. The best part of school is my friends. The school part of school that's best is, well, I mean, some classes are okay. I know, my best class is band. It's really cool.

Shawn: I know. Band is the best class. I hated it at first when we got the new band director. First day of class he plays Beethoven really loud. Some of the students almost ran out. A few smiled and really seemed to like it. Then he played some classical guitar music. I loved it. Then he played some music from when he was in college. I'd heard it on oldies stations. He shocked us when he played music from some bands we like. Then he played something else.

Tasha: I remember. He played that electronic version of Beethoven's music. So it was like time travel with music. It was so much fun. We did this huge project with different types of music that we picked. One from each of the past few centuries. I'd never heard Civil War songs or World War songs.

Shawn: Yeah, music is something I'm really interested in. I like band class a lot. Now if my other classes had music in them that would get me going. My science teacher in middle school used a guitar once to show how sound waves work. I remember that. I think it was my ninth grade English teacher who used words from songs to teach poetry. That was great.

Tasha: I know another good class. Sociology. I mean, what is sociology? It shows up on my schedule for second semester of tenth grade. There was nothing else to take. I really liked it. The teacher was so different. She taught sociology by making the people in our class the society we studied and analyzed. Then when we read the textbook we just saw how everything related to us. The best ever was when we imagined ourselves coming back for our twenty-fifth high school reunion. My boyfriend then was in the class, so when it was my turn I talked about how he and I were married right after college, we had two children who were now in high school, and I was a lawyer and my husband was a stay at home dad who ran an Internet business. My boyfriend got all embarrassed at first but then got into it. He told everyone how he loved being the stay at home dad. It was so funny.

Shawn: Sports are good. I go to some games. Clubs are fine for people who like that stuff. I don't get into clubs. Aren't you on the academic team, Tasha?

Tasha: Yeah. It's hard work. We practice all the time, but I love winning those competitions. Our coach says it will help us get into good colleges. I just think it's fun, like a television game show.

Tasha and Shawn talk about people when they talk about what is good at school. Their friends are at the top of the list for favorite people at school. Teachers who make school interesting are mentioned positively. No laws, policies, bureaucratic regulations, or political promises are mentioned by Tasha and Shawn. Students live at the classroom level. Discussions about education laws, policies, and regulations may lead to decisions that impact classrooms, but many of the people involved in those decisions or discussions do not know Tasha or Shawn or work with Tasha and Shawn. Teachers in classrooms know Tasha and Shawn. If your goal is to directly, significantly, and personally impact Tasha and Shawn's education you have to be where that education happens—in classrooms with Tasha and Shawn. Education laws, policies, and regulations change with new political trends, new societal or demographic trends, new government philosophies, new leadership or new court decisions. What matters most in Tasha and Shawn's education that educators can almost totally control is what happens in classrooms. That opportunity to control the most important of all variables within the authority of educators confirms that despite the cynical cries of contemptuous critics who consistently claim "that will never work," teachers who daily touch lives in magnificently important ways can confidently respond. Their accurate and certain reply can be, "Yes it does work. Come to my classroom and watch it work. In my classroom students learn. In my classroom there are no limits to learning. Come watch and then go do what you see us doing or better yet, go do it better than we are and tell me how you did that." How could the teacher in classroom 317 borrow an idea from the teacher in classroom 318 and improve it? One way is to adjust the idea to match the unique wholesome strengths, goals, knowledge, talents, interests, and curiosities of the students in classroom 317 with the new teaching idea to personalize the learning activity.

A lesson can be learned from capitalism. Automobile manufacturers sell a large variety of cars. The range expands from the smallest economy car to the most elaborate luxury car, from a gasoline saving hybrid engine model to a gasoline thirsty truck or sport utility vehicle. The range of products is intended to fully satisfy the range of needs and wants across all consumers. Food producers, fashion designers, shoe manufacturers, cosmetic makers, music companies, movie producers, and other businesses offer consumers an endlessly expanding range of product choices. Even products that have been successful for years are updated with improvements as consumers develop new needs, wants, and preferences. One style or one size car, coat, shoe, cosmetics, music, or movie does not fit all consumers.

One style or size of classroom instructional activity does not fit the needs of every student day after day, year after year. This year's students are a different group with different life experiences, ideas, strengths, and needs than last year's students. A repeat of what was done last year will not maximize learning. A repeat of what was done last year also denies the teacher the immensely rewarding experience of getting to know the students, of designing uniquely effective instructional activities for those students based on personalized knowledge of them, and of seeing extraordinary student achievement result from the time and effort invested in the process of causing learning.

The "but that will never work" chorus of "can't wait to retire" cynics, the "how long until summer vacation" naysayers or "I taught them but they did not learn" dissemblers will find perpetual excuses such as the following:

- But you don't know the students I teach—they are impossible.
- Families just don't care anymore.
- Parents always believe what their children tell them about school.
- If students did their homework they would pass. I can't do the work for them.
- All those new laws and policies keep me from doing my job.

- The students expect to be entertained. School is work, not entertainment.
- How can you teach students who come to school dressed for a party, using their cell phone, and listening to awful music on their new pocket size music machine?
- Do families do anything? We feed students breakfast and lunch. We babysit before and after school. We give them clothes. No wonder some students never work. They think school is a free restaurant or toy store.
- I've been doing it this way for twenty-three years and that's not going to change.
- Who has the time to do any new lesson plans? We bought textbooks. The books come with other materials. That's what we use.
- I never call parents. I used to but they blamed me for everything or they lied to cover up for their child. They were so difficult to deal with. I just quit. They can call me. They can show some interest. I just really resent people who cannot do my job telling me how to do my job. I'd love to see some of those people who get quoted in the newspaper come into my classroom and teach for a week. They would never last one day.

Extreme students are created, nurtured, encouraged, challenged, and guided by teachers who make no excuses, by teachers who think it is their duty to find a way to cause learning, and by teachers who know the students well enough to know how to make them extreme students.

Why is it so important for students to become extreme students? Students deserve to learn as much and as well as possible. Students deserve the very best. That is reason enough.

Textbooks are to vibrant mental activity what television is to vibrant physical activity. Wait a minute, Keen, a person who is watching television is sitting down, not physically active. That is correct. A student who is reading or just looking at the typical middle school or high school textbook is not vibrantly mentally active. The typical page in a common textbook may have the impact on a student's brain that a television screen picture has on a viewer's brain, which is minimal in terms of learning, thinking, wondering, analyzing, and reflecting.

Perhaps the ultimate statement of "but that will never work" comes each day from students who make limited effort in response to the habitual routine of textbook pages, worksheets, videos, lectures, and tests on Friday. Students who fail, students who make low grades, students who work and think and learn yet could do much more sophisticated and challenging learning are daily defaulting to a "but that will never work" response that takes them to (1) do nothing, (2) do enough to pass, (3) do enough to be academically eligible for sports, (4) do enough to stay out of trouble at home, (5) do enough to get into college or vocational technical school or to just graduate and get out, or (6) do enough to earn a college scholarship.

Are the current results in education acceptable? On a macro scale the answer is no. Studies, reports, listings, think tank documents, presidential speeches, media stories communicate perpetual concerns. This traffic jam of noise results in conservatives accusing public schools of malfunction and liberals accusing conservatives of mischievous motives. Away from that continuing debate, teachers and students go to school. On that micro scale, on that personal and interpersonal scale in classrooms, there is a range of brilliant work being done where dynamic teaching is causing extraordinary learning to the opposite, where pedantic routines impose brain death–defying drudgery on students and teachers. A logical response to that micro reality is to identify the brilliant work, understand it, and apply it. The solidly established research listed in this book about characteristics of great teachers and the newly established research presented in this book about characteristics of extreme students are intended for such practical, vital, and powerful purposes.

❖

"Are you on your way to class?" Mrs. Phillips asked the only student who was in the hallway about one minute after sixth period class had begun.

"Yeah. I have a note," he said with confidence of a diplomat whose credentials provide immunity.

"What class do you have now?" Mrs. Phillips asked as they walked.

"Language arts, Ms. Phillips," he answered politely.

"Well, what are you going to learn in language arts?" Mrs. Phillips inquired.

With no pause at all, he stated, "Whatever she's teaching."

Without meaning to be profound, the student may have suggested a fundamental truth. For most students, their learning experience at school is defined by, designed by, controlled by, and provided by their teachers. If boundaries on learning are established it may be because the student has translated the messages of many years of school into this conclusion—teachers tell you what to do, you do it, you pass, you get summer off, then you do more of the same again until eventually it's over and you can go do something you are interested in. To truly educate students, the conscientious observer would reply, "But those limits and routines will never work well." People who recall their best teachers know that those great teachers inspired limitless thinking and challenged students to do meaningful work. Those great teachers required mastery of the basics yet encouraged exploration of the frontier of ideas, creativity, questions, imagination, and thought. Those teachers discovered what worked in the classroom and worked with students in fascinating ways to jointly discover ways to learn.

In the early years of childhood much learning occurs through a guided discovery process. An adult and a child gaze at the stars, watch a puppy play, notice a flower in spring, identify rules of safety, talk about how friends treat each other, play a game and see how it works, bake cookies together and watch the change from a bowl of dough to a cookie jar filled with treats. This guided discovery adventure far too often fades away in the school process of education, but that is not necessary. The wonder about and the inclination toward discovery is within each student and each teacher.

How does a teacher become an educator who fully inspires and nurtures the wholesome intellectual curiosity for knowledge within students? Make your students a topic of your wholesome intellectual curiosity for knowledge. Know those students, know how they learn, know what their wholesome knowledge base includes, know about their wholesome talents and interests. Design learning activities that connect what students bring to class with what they need to learn. Make students a topic about which you are an extreme student.

Also, continue to be an extreme student of the subjects you teach. Continuing to learn about your teaching area reminds you of the demands of, the joys of, the work involved in, and the possible frustrations in the learning process. If you take a graduate school class and you mentally evaluate how the class is being taught, use that reflection as a way to think as a student thinks. How do your students see the experience they are having in your classroom?

Be a person who in school and away from school fully develops and pursues wholesome intellectual curiosities for knowledge about teaching, learning, students, hobbies, interests, knowledge, and talents.

Teachers who inspire and nurture extreme students are teachers who themselves are extreme students, continually experiencing and applying extreme learning about students and about life.

Well-intentioned, politically motivated, or otherwise energized reformers of education sometimes emphasized "systemic reform" as the essential element in educational improvement. The hope is that if the long elusive perfect central office reorganization, state department office of education restructuring, or federal department of education reengineering could be implemented then with a newly efficient and effective bureaucratic system all students would, at long last, succeed at school. Of course, helpful and wise laws, policies, regulations, reforms, and organizational structures can support schools; however, of all the ideas in education that do deserve a response of "but that will never work" it is possible that the inflated expectations of systemic, organizational, political, bureaucratic reform are most deserving of that response. Higher efficiency and increased effectiveness in the bureaucracy of education are helpful, but those enhancements may have no direct impact on Tasha and Shawn. Systemic, political reforms do not directly cause learning. Great teaching, effective teaching, extreme teaching done in classrooms interpersonally between teachers and students causes learning.

The most recent effort in the systemic reform evolution is the federal government's No Child Left Behind (NCLB) act. The Tenth Amendment to the U.S. Constitution explains that powers not assigned to the national government or not denied to the state governments belong to the states. Supporters of NCLB may cite other constitutional language, legal precedent, or Supreme Court opinions, but the facts remain: (1) education is a state responsibility carried out through local school districts, and (2) states and communities can do a much better job with education than the national government can.

We move now to consideration of an emerging question. If systemic reform is limited in its impact, where should educational reform efforts be directed, and where and how will educational results most effectively be improved?

Chapter 6

The Classroom Community

There is no perfect, ideal bureaucratic system for education. Systems can be improved in efficiency and effectiveness, but superior student achievement is not primarily a function of systemic, bureaucratic processes. Learning is not bureaucratic, meaning that a push in or from the bureaucratic system does not necessarily result in a student achievement pull in the classroom.

There can be ideal classrooms that create classroom communities in which extreme students are created, inspired, nurtured, and challenged. In these classroom communities, teachers and students limitlessly learn with and from each other. Rather than describe this classroom community, let's visit two of them and then contrast them with two classrooms that are quite different.

✛

Ms. Morton looked around her seventh grade language arts classroom with a sense of pride and accomplishment. Everything looked exactly right. She had stayed on Friday for an hour or so after school to make sure that when students walked into the classroom on Monday morning they would notice a completely different appearance to the room.

The old posters had been removed. Ms. Morton had accumulated and put on the walls poster after poster for years. It seemed that every August when she returned to school there was a mailbox full of posters waiting for her. Various organizations sent posters to promote reading, encourage learning another language, discourage use of tobacco products, support volunteering in the community, encourage physical exercise, and report crimes or related misconduct anonymously to a local number. The posters communicated well-intentioned and important messages, but they all looked alike. Whoever designed them apparently did not spend much time with seventh graders, because the posters were just so plain. Seventh graders are anything but plain. So Ms. Morton removed the old posters.

What inspired Ms. Morton to dramatically redesign the classroom? At her church the prior Sunday the music director had made an unprecedented change in the music selections for the worship service. All of the songs used in the first half of the service were majestic musical treasures of the past several centuries. Several hymns of the faithful from the seventeenth through the nineteenth centuries were selected to stir the souls, touch the hearts, and awaken important memories of the older half of the congregation. All of the songs used in the second half of the service were as contemporary as this morning's sunrise. The younger half of the congregation—especially students in middle school, high school, or college—responded to these songs with pep rally enthusiasm. The large projection screen broadcast videos and the contemporary songs communicated messages that were amazingly similar to the songs used earlier in the service, but the preferred style, the lively atmosphere, the impact on the younger members of the church intrigued Ms. Morton.

The pastor preached a fascinating sermon about the timeless truths taught through the centuries by the church and how important it is to teach those truths in ways that can be understood. His sermon included a skit of two parents and their three teenagers deciding where to go out for supper: an old-fashioned family style home cooking favorite or a new restaurant featuring international menus, organic foods, or vegetarian delicacies. They decided on a buffet restaurant known for its variety of traditional favorites and contemporary culinary creations.

The sermon also included two audio selections. One was from a radio soap opera from the 1930s. The dialogue was formal yet amusing. The other was from a satellite radio system that provided over one hundred choices of programming selections. The younger members had never heard a 1930s broadcast. The satellite radio system was new to some of the older members.

Then the preacher spoke in Spanish for about six minutes. Perhaps 5 percent of the people in the congregation no matter what their age could understand what was being said. The conclusion of the sermon, spoken in English, projected on the video screen and rapped by a well-rehearsed cross-section of nine church members ranging in age from eight to eighty-three was "People understand when you speak their language." Ms. Morton decided she had to speak the language of seventh graders to fully inspire, instruct, connect with, and cause learning by seventh graders.

Ms. Morton did not begin wearing the clothes seventh graders prefer, but she did spend time in clothing stores seventh graders like. She did not begin listening to the music of seventh graders, but she did become more aware of that music. She did not start watching the top ten favorite television programs of seventh graders, but she did begin watching one of those middle school favorites. She decided to pick a different television show from the favorite list for viewing each week. Ms. Morton did not start eating pizza whenever possible, although she knew it was the favorite food of seventh graders. She did promise herself to visit the school cafeteria on the weekly pizza day to see and hear the reactions to that ultimate food of choice of teenagers. She did not begin to punctuate her speech pattern with the latest words that seventh graders used, but she decided to create a weekly spelling test that included the new meanings of old words, but the old spelling still was required. If the word "sweet" once meant a sugary taste but now described a fantastic dunk in a basketball game, an amazing new electronic gadget's ability to contain and play thousands of songs or other very favorable events or results, she would use that to show how vibrant language is.

So, on Monday morning as seventh graders walked into Ms. Morton's class, a few noticed the different look of the room but said nothing. Others, if they noticed at all, had a short reaction such as "looks different" or "something changed." Two or three students were very observant and very impressed. They told Mrs. Morton that the room looked cool. One student was heard saying she liked the old way better.

What exactly had Ms. Morton used to redesign the room and how did the new design look? Donations. She had asked her students to list their three favorite businesses in town. Restaurants, clothing stores, music stores, large electronic stores, electronic game cafés, or arcades, coffee shops, sports facilities, movie theaters, and more. She then called many of these businesses to ask for donations of posters, logos, menus, hats, T-shirts, promotional materials, displays, product samples, coupons, signs, and more. Almost all of the stores she called were glad to provide materials, much of which they would have thrown away. Ms. Morton's classroom resembled the outfield wall of a minor league baseball park where every square foot of space has been sold to an advertiser. The classroom walls made it look more like a three-dimensional advertisement for a new shopping mall. If the new decor was an advertisement for anything, it was for more quantity and more quality in the learning of seventh grade language arts by all students. The items donated were also an advertisement for partnerships. Local businesses were generous with their donations. One parent, one guardian, and one retired teacher—each of whom had often told Ms. Morton, "Let me know when I can help"—gladly made most of the phone calls to the businesses, picked up the donations, and delivered everything to Ms. Morton's school. Ms. Morton spent no money and little time on this project. Two high school students who had to take a community service class helped set up the classroom decor on Friday after school.

First period class on this eventful Monday morning began with this statement by Ms. Morton to her twenty-seven young scholars. "Good morning. Welcome to a new week at school. You'll notice that the room is decorated quite differently than it was on Friday." Heads turned, smiles were noticed, favorable comments were made, and two students applauded. "Now, for the next three minutes, please write a description of how the room looks now, what is different, which design you prefer, and why you prefer it."

Those three minutes were filled with continuous thinking and willing writing. No cries of "that's too hard" or "that's too much to do" or "how do I get started?" Everyone began promptly and everyone worked throughout the time allocated to the writing activity. Ms. Morton made individual contact with most students as she walked through the classroom during the three minutes. Her frequent statements of "good idea," "very well explained," "neat thinking," "that's so creative," and "excellent" were the only sounds heard although a silent smile followed each of her encouraging comments.

What had the students noticed? Ms. Morton was eager for the students to hear from each other and to realize that different people looking at the same visual articles could write very different observations about what had been seen.

Ms. Morton was pleased that the students wrote so eagerly. The new design of and appearance of the classroom had now aroused some real curiosity among the students. They were carefully noticing the details of the new decor and they were stretching their memories to recall the prior appearance. In their writings, Ms. Morton pleasantly noticed that some students were asking how, what, and why questions about the classroom changes. The students were observing, thinking, analyzing, evaluating, wondering, and that contemplation was leading to some insightful writing. The sentences and paragraphs were purposeful with organization of thoughts into well-designed writing pieces. Some students left their desks for a closer, detailed reading of particular signs, posters, displays, and other items as if they were archaeologists examining artifacts that could reveal previously perplexing secrets of an ancient culture. Ms. Morton smiled as she saw the students intently read the materials around the classroom and reread their own writing. The students were paying precise scientific-style attention, having been captured by the power of fascination to figure out exactly what was going on in their classroom. Ms. Morton confidently let the original allotment of three minutes expand to five minutes because every student was abiding by the school's three rules for academic success: work, work more, keep working.

At the end of five minutes Ms. Morton acknowledged the impressive effort each student had made. "It's quite possible that no two of your answers are exactly alike, but that what each of you wrote makes perfect sense. Keep that idea in mind—two people looking at the same collection of materials, reading the same information or ideas can reach very real, yet very different conclusions. Let's hear your ideas about what has changed in our classroom and about which design you prefer. Good, Brad, you start, please. Then Monica and Gayle."

Brad liked to have an audience, so he performed with great ease and confidence. "Everything in this classroom that could change has changed. We still have desks and books, of course, but we have a very cool classroom makeover. I like the new design much better than the old look. The new way is so much more colorful and, you know, so much more fun to look at. I wrote a lot more than that, but the main thing is that it doesn't look like a classroom any more. It looks like some place I want to go."

Several students laughed as did Ms. Morton. At long last there was a classroom that Brad wanted to be in. Ms. Morton knew that she had heard something quite important from Brad, and she correctly concluded that his idea was shared by other students.

Monica read the last paragraph of her paper aloud. "I'm going to ask my parents if I can decorate my room at home the way Ms. Morton decorated our classroom. It would be so exciting for my room to look like my favorite stores. This could be the start of my career as a very rich and famous interior decorator."

Gayle was next. "What really surprises me is that I just don't remember a lot about what the room used to look like. I'm in this classroom every day, but I never really noticed much. Maybe there wasn't much to really notice. The new stuff is so cool. I'm noticing everything now."

Across the hall in another seventh grade language arts class, these instructions are written on the front marker board: Turn to page 171 in the writing book. Read pages 171 and 172. Complete the exercises on page 173." Mr. Robbins, the teacher, added these words of spoken guidance: "For question four on page 173, be sure to look at the U.S. flag in the corner before you answer. They ask you to tell what you see and think when you look at a U.S. flag. Then they ask you to tell what you notice that is different about another flag. So, I brought in one of our school flags from the library. Any questions? Okay, I'll give you thirty minutes to do that work and then we'll take the chapter 13 pretest if the volunteer office worker gets back with the test copies I asked her to make."

In which of these two classrooms is it more likely that students will learn? In which of these two classrooms will the characteristics of extreme students be developed, applied, nurtured, and challenged? As you reflect on those questions, please use the list of extreme student characteristics as a guide:

1. Extreme students are curious in a healthy, lively, purposeful way and thrive in school when their curiosities are connected with what they are learning.
2. Extreme students ask questions.
3. Extreme students are active within their own minds.
4. Extreme students are organized.
5. Extreme students read, read, and read.
6. Extreme students pay attention with total concentration.
7. Extreme students work hard.

Ms. Morton has designed a classroom atmosphere and environment that has energized student curiosity. The writing task she gave her students invites questioning, thinking, creativity, analysis, and wonder within the minds of students as they write and between the minds of all students as they present, trade, and consider everyone's ideas. The classroom is organized, which helps provide an organized plan for the students. The students are reading and may read more as they become further fascinated with today's activity. Students are willingly paying attention to their work because the activity has intrigued them, fascinated them, increased their curiosity, connected with their real lives, and connected with their wholesome knowledge, interests, or talents. The quantity of and the quality of learning that Ms. Morton and her students will experience together, will create together, and will share is unlimited. The teacher and the students will learn with one another and from one another. Ms. Morton will professionally guide the input, the questions, the ideas, and the work from students to ensure that the lesson objectives are achieved and each student masters the objectives. The students will realize that their intellectual contribution to the class is valued, is taken seriously, is appreciated, and is important. The students and Ms. Morton will "communitize" their learning meaning that they will rely on, learn from, learn with, and cooperate with each other. Each person will still do his or her work; however, the totality of learning will expand as each person contributes to the learning of everyone. The result can be a classroom community of extreme students led by a very proud and productive extreme teacher.

Let's return to Ms. Morton's classroom. All students completed their writing. Three students have spoken to share their ideas. What activities would you do next to build upon and apply the very solid initial activities of today's lesson in Ms. Morton's classroom? Either below or on separate paper, please write the rest of the lesson plan as you would complete what Ms. Morton and her students have begun.

1.
2.
3.
4.

Perhaps you thought of ideas such as these:

1. Have each of the other students who had not yet spoken give a sentence or two that summarized which classroom design they liked better and why. The results could be tabulated and analyzed.
2. Expand the classroom redesign idea to the entire school building. What suggestions would the students make to improve the appearance of the interior of the school building?
3. Evaluate why some students liked the new design. Or, if everyone liked the same design, what variety of reasons did they offer?
4. Discuss with students what conclusions can be reached as they realize that while everyone was looking at the same classroom design, no two evaluations of the classroom makeover were identical. Relate this to how different readers may react differently to a short story, a poem, a novel, or a biography.

5. Create a magazine with the title "Classroom Makeover." Give the students the requirements—front cover, number of articles, number of advertisements, table of contents, letters to the editor—as a creative way to explore the writing process.

Perhaps your ideas are completely different from the five possibilities listed above. That is part of the adventure of education. It is unlikely that you included on your list an activity similar to what Mr. Robbins imposed on his students. The ordinary, superficial, prefabricated tasks that Mr. Robbins gave his students are painfully finite. If any learning results from the redundant routine he uses daily, it is limited to what textbook pages and exercises can accomplish as they are mechanically read and completed—or not read and copied, or not read and not done—by students. Mr. Robbins is a spectator in his classroom. The students are visitors in the classroom. There is very little interaction of minds, ideas, or people. It is interesting to watch Mr. Robbins later in the day when he performs his duties as an assistant coach of a swimming team. If he taught his classes with the energy, the commitment, the variety of activities, the individualized attention, the personal interaction that he always includes at swim practice, where he expects his team to work as an athletic community of mutually dedicated overachievers, the results could be extraordinary.

Can a classroom community be established in a high school? The answer, of course, is yes. We will visit Mr. Marion's twelfth grade United States government class to discover that a high school classroom community with students who are very eager to finish high school and whose "senioritis" is more obvious each day can still be sufficiently fascinated by learning to build extreme student skills.

⁘

"Good morning. Lights. Camera. Action. We begin today with a short portion of a major motion picture, well, actually, it is the final two minutes of our school's basketball game from two nights ago. Our girls' team took their 14-3 record across town and emerged with a highly competitive 64-62 overtime win. As we watch the final two minutes, which I edited to avoid time-outs or other stops in the game, please pay very close attention to the referees. Notice what they watch and think about how they make their decisions."

The students paid total attention throughout the two minutes. There were cheers for great shots made and grumbling about a particular call by one referee. The attention level was high whether it was from a student who had attended the game in person or not, whether from a student who liked basketball a lot or was not interested in basketball at all. Watching two minutes of a high school girls' basketball game that included people they knew captured the students' interest.

Before Mr. Marion could ask the first question, three students had raised their hands showing an urgency to respond to the video. "Brian, what's on your mind?" Mr. Marion asked with a sincere smile that expressed his satisfaction that students were thinking.

"That call was so bad. She had established her position in the paint. She was playing perfect defense. The other player charged into her. I talked to Emily about that call. She knows it was a bad call, but she could not risk arguing with the referee. It was so cool that Emily hit our next shot and blocked their next shot after that."

"You could be a good sports broadcaster, Brian. Let's see what Julie thinks and then we'll hear from Robert. Your turn, Julie."

"I watched the referees like you said to. I wondered if the referee who made that call was in the right place. She seemed to be far away from the place where that player ran into Emily." Several students nodded their heads to agree with Julie's comment. Robert spoke next.

"Free throws were so important. We hit six free throws out of six tries in the last two minutes. So, the referees were calling fouls on the other team, too. But hitting those free throws made a huge difference."

Mr. Marion's class is about U.S. government with an emphasis on political science and some consideration of economics, including how government policies can impact the economy. The class spent a lot of time reading, discussing, and explaining the U.S. Constitution using Supreme Court opinions, the original debates in 1787 and 1788, plus current newspaper and website articles of events that showed issues and questions associated with the Constitution now. How does a high school basketball game connect with the curriculum of the U.S. government class? Please think about that and below or on separate paper list your thoughts.

-
-
-
-

Societies and communities, acting through governments, enact laws. High school basketball games, participated in by teams from schools that are governed by a state athletic commission or other governing authority, have rules.

Police officers and courts enforce laws and resolve legal disputes. Referees of high school basketball games enforce the rules of basketball. Local, regional, or state athletic agencies can help resolve disputes related to sports.

Societies establish standards for privileges and responsibilities. There are age requirements to obtain a driver's license, to vote, to sign a contract, or to hold elective office. A school and/or an athletic governing agency can establish academic and other requirements for student participation in athletics.

The Fourteenth Amendment to the U.S. Constitution affirms the importance of equal protection of the law and due process of law. In that same spirit, a high school could hold tryouts for a basketball team with all qualified students having equal opportunity to compete for selection to the team. The coach could explain to everyone the objective, measured, skills-based, results-based, quantifiable process for selection of team members. Accurately followed selection criteria could help provide equal opportunity and equal protection to all students who try out for the team.

Governments maintain, monitor, analyze, and apply many statistics. Demographic trends, tax revenues, policies, laws, government spending, and budget decisions are impacted by statistics. Basketball teams can analyze statistics from games to identify what is working and what needs to improve.

The First Amendment protects the right of citizens to peaceably assemble. Similarly, students may attend a high school basketball game, but if their conduct at the game became disorderly they could be required to leave. The First Amendment protects freedom of speech, but a high school player or coach who speaks to a basketball referee in unacceptable ways could be removed from the game.

Back in Mr. Marion's classroom, he distributed an index card to each student. The distribution was done randomly. The cards had one number per card. The numbers ranged from 1 to 27. Each student had a different number. Mr. Marion then asked, "Let's imagine that you would like to attend the next basketball game at our school. The price is usually $3 for a student, but that will change this time. The price you will pay is equal in dollars to the number I just gave you. Now there is a deal. You may bring a friend free. In fact you may bring two friends free. So, how many of you would support this new plan?" Eight hands went up. Those students were asked to tell the number on their card. The numbers were 1,2,3,4,5,6,7 and 8. The student with number 9 explained that she never went to basketball games so it did not matter to her, but she did think that this method was unfair and would reduce attendance. She added, "Wouldn't this be illegal or something?"

After a heated debate over the ticket pricing change, Mr. Marion tried a different application. "Okay. We'll keep the three dollar admission price, since that is fair to everyone. But going to the concession stand is optional. If we let you attend the game for the same price as everyone else, why do we have to charge everyone the same prices at the concession stand? So, put a zero after the number on your index card. Your 1 becomes a 10. The 27 becomes 270. The price of a large soft drink will range from 10 cents to $2.70 depending on your card. When you get your soft drink you turn in the card so nobody else can use it. How's this system sound to you?"

The debate was loud and lively but orderly. Conclusions were clear that this system was unfair. Mr. Marion then had the student with 1 on the index card trade with the student who had 27 on the index card. Other changes were made so students got the opposite card of what they started with. Mr. Marion explained the next questions.

"To build excitement at the game there is a contest at halftime. If your card has 1 on it, you get to take a shot at the basket from one foot away. Hit the shot and you win $1. The person with 27 on the card takes a shot from 27 feet away and would win $27 if the shot goes in. Is this fair?"

The amazing part of the discussion was that most students said they would like to be number 12, 13, or 14. Those shots would not be too far away and the money was good. It was a lot more money than $1 and it was a lot more possible to hit the shot than from twenty-seven feet. The idea of compromise in a political system was then discussed. The students decided that the best plan would be to select randomly the students who could take a halftime shot for money, but let each person decide the length of the shot knowing the value and the difficulty would increase together as the number increased.

Mr. Marion then led the students in some discussion about the topics of class so far. He then asked, "Who won the game we watched the two minute conclusion of?" Several students replied, "We did." Mr. Marion said, "I know it looks that way, but only if you count the points one at a time. Our team was ahead at halftime 32-26. The game was tied at the end of the second half, 54-54. Then we scored 10 points in the overtime and the other team scored 8 points. You are right, we won. But look at the statistics closely. Which team shot a better percentage in each category?

Mr. Marion had written the statistics on the front marker board before class (see table 6.1). They had not been given much attention until now. As Mr. Marion and the students did the math, it was obvious that the other team had better percentages in free throws—67 percent to 50 percent, in two-point shots—50 percent to 42 percent, and in three-point shots—40 percent to 33 percent.

Ellen spoke up. "But it's not the percentages that matter. The winner is the team with the most points. Sure, teams try to hit high percentages, but it's points that count."

Mr. Marion and the class listened to a few other comments and opinions. Then Mr. Marion asked this question. "You are right. The only fair way to count points in basketball is to count each point. The team with more points wins. Why don't we use that system of counting in our presidential elections? That election is all about percentages in each state and in the District of Columbia. Fifty-one different elections with the winner taking all of a state's electoral votes if he or she has the largest percentage of popular votes in that state. Please take the next four minutes of class to read pages 276 to 277 in your textbooks about presidential elections."

Table 6.1. Shooting Statistics

	Free Throws	*2-Point Shots*	*3-Point Shots*	*Total Points*
Us	10 out of 20	21 out of 50	4 out of 12	64
Them	8 out of 12	21 out of 42	4 out of 10	62

After the reading was completed, the discussion was continuous throughout the rest of class. The thinking was profound. The interaction was productive. The attention level was high. The questions were insightful. The learning was without limit. The students seemed genuinely sorry as the bell rang to end class, but Mr. Marion promised that today's adventure would continue tomorrow. He had given them their assignment, which was to read a brochure he gave everyone a copy of. The brochure was about eighteen-year-olds and their turnout as voters in elections.

In another classroom at the same school, high school seniors in a United States government class are opening their textbooks to chapter 13, "Elections in a Democracy." The chapter has many charts, lots of statistics, a few quotes from important historical leaders, an occasional set of questions, some end-of-the-chapter activities, and two long think-and-explain questions. There are pictures of former U.S. presidents on election nights. There are pictures of local and state candidates, campaign materials, and voting precincts. The information is accurate. The students were assigned to read the chapter for today and write an outline of the chapter in the first half of class today. The second half of class would be filled with a video, *The Right to Vote: Changes from 1789 to 2001.* If any time was left after the video, the teacher and the students would review important vocabulary terms that were used in the textbook and in the video. The teacher, Ms. Asberry, was a likable, polite, friendly faculty member whose twenty-four years at the school were twenty-three years of reruns of her first year. A new textbook or changing from filmstrips or movies to video cartridges had been the major adjustments in her routines over the years, now the decades. She had watched students come and go for twenty-four years. Her students had watched textbook chapters and filmstrips/movies/videos come and go for years. School should be much more for students and for teachers than a daily repetitive sequence of come and go.

In what ways did Mr. Marion's class create, nurture, inspire, challenge, and develop the characteristics of extreme students? In the space below or on separate paper, please write your reflections on that question. The characteristics are listed with space to add your thoughts so the author and reader can interact and create our version of a classroom community.

1. Extreme students are curious in a very healthy, lively, purposeful way and thrive in school when their curiosities are connected with what they are learning.

2. Extreme students ask questions.

3. Extreme students are active within their own minds.

4. Extreme students are organized.

5. Extreme students read, read, and read.

6. Extreme students pay attention with total concentration.

7. Extreme students work hard.

The sense of community, the feeling of community, the experience of community can be established in many ways that build valued interaction, build a shared commitment to a mutually beneficial result, and build the realization that we are in this together. How did the learning activities in Mr. Marion's classroom help establish a classroom community? What could he do to further establish a classroom community? How did the learning activities in Ms. Asberry's classroom help establish a classroom community? What could she do to better establish a classroom community?

Your turn, but first please seriously think about what your idea of teaching is. Think also about what your idea of a teacher is. Permit yourself to be genuine, so avoid stale, forced terminology that might appear on charts used by school administrators when they make formal observations in classrooms. Those charts have page after page of grids and boxes to indicate whether certain tasks were done or certain traits were noticed. Those forms serve a purpose, but they do not serve our purpose at this moment. Our intention is for you to explain your idea of teaching and your idea of a teacher. Please give yourself ample time to think and to write.

My idea of teaching:

My idea of a teacher:

Notice that in this activity we did not use the term "job description" of a teacher although that needs to be understood by all educators in a school. We also did not use the observation forms from the Human Resources Department of a school district although those forms are official documents. We used the mind to ponder the idea of teaching and the idea of a teacher.

For example, the idea of space travel is different from the scientific functions of rockets and the rigorous training of astronauts; the idea of space travel includes discovery, adventure, expanding the frontier, removing limits, courage, wonder, questions to answer, curiosities to explore, thinking to do, and much hard work. The idea of an astronaut is similarly dynamic, so while building on a foundation of specifically acquired skills it is more than the total of those skills.

Thoughts about the idea of teaching could range from "motivate students" to "provide opportunities for everyone to learn," from "develop each student's potential" to "carry out the required curriculum" and many other possibilities. From an idea of teaching would logically flow a related idea of a teacher. From that idea of a teacher would emerge the day to day activities that a teacher designs, organizes, implements, and evaluates to carry out the ideas of what teaching is and of what a teacher is.

The idea of teaching that creates, nurtures, inspires, challenges, guides, leads, interacts with, and encourages extreme students is teaching that causes learning about topics and through classroom activities, with students eager to and able to learn more. The idea of a teacher who creates, nurtures, inspires, challenges, guides, leads, interacts with, and encourages extreme students is of a teacher who designs, organizes, implements, and evaluates learning activities and experiences that (1) cause students to use and develop the seven characteristics of extreme students and (2) create a classroom community.

Now it is your turn to design a classroom learning activity that will cause students to use and develop the seven characteristics of extreme students and will create a classroom community. Think about what you teach and who you teach. Design a real lesson that you can use. Borrow ideas from your best teachers, from your best teaching, from the examples of superior teaching in Ms. Morton's classroom and Mr. Marion's classroom. Think of the worst teaching you endured as a student and ask yourself what the opposite of that would be. Think of great teaching ideas you have studied or read about on your own or heard about. Use some separate paper, use the format that works best for you, use the best possible ideas, and design the best possible lesson.

To self-evaluate the lesson you designed, see in what ways the lesson (1) makes connections between the wholesome knowledge, interests, and talents of students and what you intend those students to learn, (2) develops in your students the seven characteristics of extreme students, and (3) applies the four characteristics of great teachers—use a variety of methods and activities; are enthusiastic about students and teaching; challenge students; make connections between today's learning and the real lives that students are living today.

You may ask, How can I design one lesson with all of those instructional elements and activities? Perhaps it will be a series of lessons that require several days to cause the intended learning and to include all of the elements of great teaching and of developing extreme students. Another question could be, How can a lesson plan show that I would be enthusiastic about teaching and about students? One part of the answer is within our conscience. Is this a fascinating lesson, is this a sequence of varied learning activities, is this a challenging experience, is this going to connect today's learning with today's real lives that students are living and bring with them into the classroom as vibrant human resources and intellectual resources, is this lesson going to cause the students and the teacher to interactively learn from one another and with one another? If we honestly answer yes to most or all of those questions, then this is a lesson that should evoke our enthusiasm. It is commonly acknowledged that students quickly and accurately determine how excited about and how dedicated to teaching a teacher is. Some students respond to teachers with the same level of excitement, enthusiasm, commitment, and involvement that the teacher offers to students. These instructional and interpersonal advantages are available to all teachers.

Teachers can quickly, easily, and personally confirm these human dynamics by remembering professional development programs they have attended. If the program included meaningful content connected with the real life you live and the real work you do as a teacher in your classroom, if the presentation was energetic, interactive, and done by a person who convinced you of their enthusiasm for the topic, for the people involved, and for the time together, the response was likely to be much more favorable.

Conversely, if the professional development is a long, monotonous lecture accompanied by prepackaged, prefabricated, generic handouts and a one-lecture-fits-all-audiences presentation, the teachers in the audience are likely to show minimal interest and experience minimal learning.

Classroom communities are built by design. Classroom communities are built as joint ventures to which each member of the community brings unique ideas, knowledge, talents, interests, skills, experience, and opinions. Classroom communities are groups of people who mutually, collectively, interactively, individually and together create, nurture, develop, and encourage the characteristics of extreme students. A classroom community is that group of students and a teacher who together are as follows:

1. Curious in a very healthy, lively way and whose individual curiosities connect with curiosities of other people in the classroom community so curiosities expand and the experience of exploring, researching, finding answers about, and identifying new questions about those curiosities is a shared endeavor. The combination of individual efforts and group efforts surpass what any one person could achieve.

2. Asking questions of each other, with each other, in response to what another classroom community member said, learned, reported, created, concluded, or discovered.

3. Active as a group within the mind of the group. Discussions in this classroom community are led by the teacher but are not only in the tennis ball sequence of teacher talks, student talks. The teacher's first question may inspire replies from several or many students who are directing ideas to each other as much or more as they are directing answers to the teacher.

4. The classroom community is organized. The teacher is the adult, the teacher is the professional, the teacher is the paid employee, the teacher is responsible for successfully implementing the approved curriculum, and the teacher is expected to design day-to-day activities that cause students to learn. Organized does not imply or require a rigid routine, but it does require substantial thinking, preparation, planning, designing, and work. There is some room for spontaneity and for embracing unexpected opportunity within an overall structure of organization; however, the overall community needs an organized and designed, managed and led process for learning as much as a community in a city or a county needs an organized and designed, managed and led process for governing, for traffic control, for police protection, for celebrations on holidays, for protection of and expression of individual rights, for protection of and decisions made about the common good. Organization that is human and humane, effective yet creative enhances community in the classroom or in cities.

5. The classroom community experiences reading, reading, and more reading. Individuals in the classroom community read materials and then discuss the reading together. The walls can be covered with quotes, ideas, vocabulary words, articles, questions to read. There are shelves with many books to help create the atmosphere that this is a frequent reading area. Students sometimes have choices of what to read. The teacher tells the students about his or her reading that applies to the class. Newspapers are used in the classroom. Students read to one another some papers they wrote themselves. Local citizens, well-known leaders, neighbors of the school, family members of the students are invited to class to read, lead a book talk, interact with students about the reading students have done.

6. In the classroom community attention is paid and concentration is total. Attention is continually directed to and attracted by fascinating learning activities that captivate students. Attention is paid to the wholesome

knowledge, talents, and interests of students especially as those can connect with what needs to be learned. Attention is paid to the leadership of the teacher and to the partnership between the teacher and the students. Attention is paid to the required curriculum and to the most effective ways to learn everything the curriculum requires. In the classroom community all resources are dedicated to meaningful learning content and meaningful learning experiences so total attention is earned, secured, maintained through the vast power of meaning. Students are eager to learn skills and content that are real now, matter now, and have meaning to the real life a student is living right now.

7. The prevailing force within the classroom community is work. The atmosphere, the activities, the creativity, the challenges, the fascination, the achievement, the relevance, the environment all inspire work and thrive on work. There are enjoyable times and there are celebrations. There are corrections and there is discipline. There is progress yet there is frustration, there is evaluation and there is change. Through it all there is the driving force of work because inaction is never productive. Purposeful, guided, organized work is fulfilling, rewarding, and renewing.

The classroom community that creates, nurtures, challenges, guides, and develops extreme students individually is itself a corporate, collective circulatory system of extreme studenting. Strange word, but that is the idea. It's as if "extreme student" is the noun and the process of becoming and then being an extreme student is described as extreme studenting. What is a teacher doing when he or she is creating the extreme student classroom community that causes students to become and then to be extreme students. You yourself live and exemplify the characteristics of an extreme student through the way you do your job. You are curious in a very healthy, lively, purposeful way about school, teaching, learning, the subjects you teach, and, above all, students. You ask questions of yourself, colleagues, students, mentors, and advisers. You are active within your mind. You are organized. You read, read, and read. You pay attention with total concentration. You work hard. The classroom community that most supports extreme students is impacted most importantly by a teacher who lives the life of an extreme student by implementing the characteristics of an extreme student minute to minute, class to class, student to student, and day to day. To create, nurture, challenge, and develop extreme students, be an extreme student yourself. Be of, by, and for the students, their learning, the curriculum, and teaching what you intend for students to be of, by, and for regarding their learning.

A question emerges, But how can I manage my classroom, keep everyone under control, teach everything the curriculum tells me I have to teach, deal with misbehaviors, grade all the papers, cope with interruptions during the day, and somehow build this wonderful classroom community? How is that possible with everything else I have to do?

Perhaps because of everything else that has to be done, the creation of a classroom community is essential because in that learning community some distractions are prevented or minimized and learning achievements are increased through cooperation toward shared goals with mutual benefits. Creating a classroom community in which a teacher and the students team up enhances classroom efficiency, effectiveness, productivity, and achievement while also increasing the commitment factor.

A few minutes after school had dismissed on a cold, snowy January Friday a smiling seventh grader walked past me as I supervised in the halls. I know how interested this student is in basketball, so earlier in the day as he went through the cafeteria serving area that I also supervise, I had asked him some questions about recent college basketball games. He had spoken with precise detail and with sophisticated analysis of basketball strategy, performance, and statistics. I pointed out the use of math in analyzing basketball games and he seemed amazed that math could be so practical. He was on his way at dismissal to middle school basketball practice. He exuberantly proclaimed, "I've got to go work hard at basketball practice." I replied, "That's what it takes." He confidently added, "To win championships it sure does."

Does that student enter a classroom saying or thinking, "I've got to work hard at math class today because that's what it takes to win a math championship"?

On that same day I spent two class periods with a sixth grade student who had been sent to the office the previous day for being disruptive in class. I sensed that the student's side of the story had some validity and I knew that misbehavior had happened. Discipline was needed, but here was a student who admitted misbehavior and behaved perfectly in the office where I had never seen her sent before.

When I heard her comments about her grades, classes, and misbehavior, an opportunity emerged to surprise her with one of my favorite questions for students who are sent to the office. Students never expect to hear this question. "Do you hate school or like school?" She said "hate" in a nano second. "Do you like anything about school?" "Yeah, I really like language arts. I like to write." I told her to report to my office the next day during the class periods she would have been in the math classes she had been removed from.

She was on time the next day. She waited calmly and patiently for me. I asked her what sports, games, or hobbies she liked. "Soccer. I really like soccer. I used to play goalie." She had told me the day before that fractions and percents were confusing to her. So, I wrote some soccer math problems for her to do. "A soccer team wins eight games and loses two games. What percent of the games were wins and what percent of the games were losses?" "You are goalie. The other team takes thirty shots in the game. You stop or block thirty shots. What percent of the shots did you block?" "If a person practices penalty kicks and they make thirty-six out of forty penalty kicks, what percentage of the kicks did they make and what percentage of the kicks did they miss?"

We Socratically discussed the soccer math after she worked on the problems for a few minutes. She answered questions correctly and was interested in the soccer aspect of our discussion. Math and soccer apparently had never connected in her mind before. Although soccer had been in her mind and math had been in her mind, she had never noticed any mental community in which soccer and math were mutually supportive, were symbiotic, were each able to improve the understanding of or skills in the other, in which soccer and math connected. Soccer is good. Math is bad. I like soccer. I hate math. Soccer makes sense. Math is stupid. Soccer is real. Math is "so who cares and when will I ever need this?" Those unspoken perspectives were changing. After an hour of very productive math work, I asked her if it all made sense. "Yeah. It's interesting because I like soccer. So, yeah, it made sense."

During that hour it became obvious that her experience with math was one of "math is the enemy." As we talked about coins and related pennies, nickels, dimes, quarters, and half dollars to fractions and to percentages, she could do the calculations. She did not see the idea of fractions or the idea of percentages. The ultimate example for students of a favorite food is pizza. Fortunately pizza slices also represent fractions and percentages. So we drew a pizza and sliced it into two large pieces each being one-half of the pizza. Those slices are too big to hold, so we sliced each half into four easy-to-hold pieces. We now have eight pieces. "Would you prefer the one-half piece or the four smaller pieces?" She thought and then said, "It's the same. I'll take the small ones since they are easy to hold." I asked her how she knew that $\frac{1}{2}$ was the same as $\frac{4}{8}$. "We drew it that way. The $\frac{1}{2}$ size never changed; we just cut it up." "Good answer. Fractions just cut something up into smaller pieces."

I asked if she knew how to cross-multiply fractions to show they are equal. A blank look was her very genuine "no" answer. "OK. $\frac{1}{2}$ equals $\frac{4}{8}$ you told me. Let's cross multiply diagonally. What's 1 times 8?" "8." "What's 2 times 4?" "8. Neat. It's the same." Even without a soccer connection, a math concept was "neat" because it had done a numerical trick that is just one of the endless tricks that numbers can do. During our time together teacher, student, math, and soccer created a classroom community. "But Keen, one on one is simple. You were working with only one student."

On that same day in the eighth grade economics class, the students and I discussed interest rates, mortgages, land value, prices of property impacted by supply and demand, the economic concept of a liquid resource, and much more. The much more was their questions or examples about property, about a family member whose property value went up, about a friend who purchased land in Arizona for a retirement home and how much that value increased. The entire group of students listened, contributed, learned, and thought. Their input was an essential resource. They learned from and with each other. We learned from and with each other.

What's the difference between textbook math, worksheet math, and soccer math? What's the difference between textbook economics, worksheet economics, and "that's like the property my uncle bought in Arizona" economics?

The student whom I worked with using soccer math was quite curious about the answers to soccer math problems because she saw herself, her life experience, her wholesome interest in soccer as part of the activity. The economics students asked questions and offered insights, all of which were taken seriously and all of which became part of our shared knowledge. The soccer math student was very active in her own mind partly because she is very good at thinking about soccer, so that thinking skill and that thinking eagerness led the way toward math thinking. The economics students are very organized. Class begins with each student opening his or her economics folder to the next line on a notebook paper page where yesterday's last idea was written. "Write the word 'liquid.' In science, in nutrition, liquid has meanings. In economics, liquid has a unique meaning. Let's figure it out. If I tell you that some money, some investments, some wealth is liquid, which do you think that means?" The initial moment in class supports very organized thinking. The soccer math student willingly read the word problems she was given. Some students dread word problems. She read them and completed them partly because to her soccer is worth reading about. The soccer math student and the economics student paid attention with total concentration and worked hard. Notice, the above sentences itemize the characteristics of extreme students. Soccer math can help nurture, inspire, even create extreme students. The soccer math student did not see herself as an extreme student, but she now has a favorable experience with and impression of herself in that scholarly category.

Is there another important overall element in the classroom community similar in importance to the characteristics of extreme students and to making connections between the wholesome knowledge, interests, and talents of students with what needs to be learned? Yes, we can call it the fascination factor. When a person is fascinated with a topic, a skill, an experience, a goal, or any other wholesome part of life, what does the person do to follow their fascination?

The fact that a person is fascinated indicates that curiosity exists. The person has questions he seeks answers to. She is active in her mind about the topic of fascination. He organizes some efforts to learn more about and to experience more with the fascination. She reads to gain new information about, understanding of, or guidance about the fascination. He pays attention to experiences, topics, and people who relate to the fascination. She works hard at efforts that connect with the fascination. People become extreme students of that which fascinates them. The fascination factor helps create, nurture, inspire, challenge, and guide extreme students.

For too many students much of school is a passive ordeal to endure. Passive because school is imposed on you and the only option is to sit through it until the day, week, semester, year, or graduation is complete. Then for an evening, weekend, vacation, summer, or lifetime you can really live, or at least you can have some selection for some involvement in what you do. There are wholesome parts of life, knowledge, and learning that do fascinate students. There are ways of exploring those fascinations that increase commitment to expertly master the topic or the skill. The advantage this gives to teachers is that students bring their fascinations, their commitments, their knowledge, interests, and talents to class with them. To help create a classroom community, to "communitize" the classroom, a teacher can lead and manage the learning activities in the classroom so the fascination factor that students bring with them is multiplied productively and purposefully. When students' fascinations are connected with the school's curriculum, the result can be the experience of unlimited learning by extreme students and the priceless rewards of causing learning by a teacher who is an extreme student of teaching, of learning, and of students.

Teachers may sometimes see themselves as the lowest ranking professional employees in the educational organization. School counselors, assistant principals, principals, central office management staff, assistant superintendents, superintendents, school board members, state education officials or bureaucrats, and federal education officials or bureaucrats may be seen as having jobs that are of higher rank in the educational power structure. Teachers have two advantages and opportunities that no other person in education has: (1) direct, continuous contact with students all day, every day and (2) the authority to be the chief executive officer (CEO) of your classroom. The purpose of a school is to cause learning. That result is impacted more by what teachers do or don't do than by another action or inaction of any other person in any other job in the corporate structure or organization of the education establishment. A teacher who thinks as, works as, and functions skillfully as the CEO of his or her classroom is a teacher who causes learning, develops extreme students, and has a profoundly meaningful career day to day, year to year, decade to decade.

Superior chief executive officers of the most successful companies listen and lead, are open-minded and decisive, seek input and provide direction, set proper examples and follow wise advice, do not claim to know it all but do require themselves to learn what they do not know and to develop talented people whose expertise in certain areas surpasses their own. There are thousands of good books about CEO skills, so readers can easily find details. For our immediate purpose, this idea is sufficient; the teacher who sees herself as CEO of her classroom knows that maximum success requires mutual commitments to each other, to shared goals, and to high standards. The most successful companies establish, create, nurture, develop, and reward a corporate community of mutually dedicated employees who care about one another, their products, their customers, and their mutual success. The teacher who thinks and works as the CEO of the classroom establishes, creates, nurtures, develops, and rewards a classroom community of students and teacher who are mutually dedicated to one another, care about one another, and care about their individual and collective success.

A successful corporate CEO does not accept the status quo as the best possible result. The teacher as classroom CEO does not accept the status quo as the best possible result. The classroom CEO creates, finds, discovers the actions that will get the desired results. The classroom CEO finds ways to maximize the skills of, the contributions of, and the achievement of each student. The teacher as classroom CEO does not find fault but exemplifies the importance of and the ways to find solutions. The teacher as chief executive officer of his classroom truly sees himself as chief education officer in his classroom. That is the most important job and the most rewarding job in education.

In anticipation of the next chapter, let's take the corporate CEO perspective one step further. The city where I was born is home to Jif peanut butter. The aroma coming from that manufacturing facility when the peanuts are being cooked is a delight to any peanut butter fan. Jif was originally called Big Top peanut butter and it was produced by a locally owned company that was founded as a successful, honorable, and generous business executive. Procter & Gamble, my original employer, purchased Big Top peanut butter, changed the name to Jif, sold the product nationally, and made significant profit by satisfying consumers. In recent years, Procter & Gamble sold Jif to Smuckers, another successful and highly respected company that is known for jelly and jam. What better food match or corporate match could there be than peanut butter and jelly?

Jif is an outstanding product. Jif is a profitable product. Why did Procter & Gamble sell it? The decision was based on several factors including an emerging awareness that Procter & Gamble could be more successful, more productive, more profitable, more efficient by applying its talents and resources toward other products. Smuckers saw Jif as a logical, harmonious, and profitable connection with its basic business. In the years since the sale, both companies involved have benefited.

If that same reasoning is applied to education, one conclusion is that similar to the fact that no one company manufactures every possible and profitable product, asking one school to maximize the educational experience of each student is not practical, efficient, or productive. The classroom community that most teachers can create to benefit most students still may not reach some students. Students who are court involved and have police records may need rehabilitation services prior to education services and may then need educational services in a unique location with specialized teachers and extraordinary measures related to security, supervision, and schedule.

Given the reality that students bring a range of abilities and life conditions to school with them, it is impractical to expect one school building and the faculty, staff, and administrators at that school to provide every possible educational, health, counseling, or related service to everyone. The student who has already spent time in juvenile jail and the student who will earn a scholarship to Harvard may need to be educated in two different schools. There are other students whose educational needs may be better met in a specialized setting. As optimistic as we should be that extreme students can be created, nurtured, inspired, and developed, it is important to be equally realistic that the educational services one school can be reasonably expected to provide cannot match the educational needs of all students. In the next chapter we briefly consider the other 5 percent of students. Dissertations, books, conferences, and data are plentiful about alternative education programs and rationales. The next chapter is not intended to match those resources but to include an important reality check that will likely grow in urgency as some societal trends grow in complexity.

Chapter 7

Successfully Educating
the Other 5 to 10 Percent

Do not run to the Fourteenth Amendment of the U.S. Constitution and shout that every student has to go the same school because of "equal protection of the law." Some students already go to alternative schools for important reasons that primarily benefit those students and secondarily benefit people at the schools those students formerly attended.

To effectively deal with the topic of the other 5 to 10 percent of students requires an explanation of who these students are and requires an urgent appeal to policy makers, political leaders, superintendents, plus other people in leadership or management positions within or impacting education. First, the appeal. On this topic, you are the CEO. Those of you who write laws, approve budgets, make policies, implement regulations, lead/manage departments of education, lead many school districts, and lead many schools, this is within your jurisdiction, your authority, your responsibility, and your expertise. This is a part of education improvement that does require systemic, structural, organizational, legal, regulatory, and policy changes.

A new law, a new policy, a new regulation usually does not immediately change the lessons planned for, the materials used in, the questions asked in, the homework given in, the tests used in, or the environment and atmosphere in a classroom. Changes in those very specific and particular actions within classrooms will result from conscientious teachers whose personal pursuit of better teaching honorably sustains their continuous improvement. Changes in those very specific and particular actions can be agreed to at the school level and can be implemented through a school's improvement plan; annual goal-setting and goal-reaching reviews; response to national, state, or local directives; test scores; or political pressures. Nonetheless, most meaningful classroom change is "bottom up," coming from the classroom CEO who takes charge of getting better

results as a personal and professional sense of duty and/or in response to improvement initiatives identified and implemented at the school level.

An individual teacher cannot create an alternative school at a different location.
Faculty colleagues alone cannot establish the criteria and the process that would
place a student in an alternative school. Teachers certainly could offer data, reports, and evidence that would support the need for alternative programs to be
created and for certain students to be placed in those alternative programs, but actions related to laws, policies, regulations, and budgets will be necessary to actually establish alternative schools and to place students in those programs. Involvement by people who make laws, policies, regulations, and budgets will be
necessary to actually establish alternative schools and to place students in those
programs. People who make laws, policies, regulations, and budgets will need to
lead the efforts on this endeavor.

Second, who are the people in this other 5 to 10 percent of students who need
educational services to be provided in an alternative school? Who are the people
in this other 5 to 10 percent of students who cannot or will not succeed in the
standard school setting, whose presence in that standard school setting interferes
with the education of other students, and whose presence in that standard school
setting is a threat to the health, safety, and work of other students and of adults at
the standard school? Some of them are what the term "extreme student" might be
presumed to mean: extreme as incorrigible, antisocial, destructive, pathological,
or criminal. The other 5 to 10 percent of students are those who cannot or will not
be productively and/or safely educated in the typical school setting.

For our purposes, the other 5 to 10 percent of students will be divided into two
groups: (1) criminal or semicriminal and (2) destructive or incorrigible. Please
adjust the percentage range of 5 to 10 percent to reflect the reality of your school,
your school district, or your state. The 5 to 10 percent range will be used here because I am aware of statistical support for that range; however, one statistic does
not fit every situation, so please modify the range to be accurate for your area of
concern or jurisdiction.

My interest in alternative education has three parts. One, the realities that are
communicated in a 1996 book I wrote, *911: The School Administrator's Guide to
Crisis Management.* Two, the persistent reality that most students do what they
are supposed to do at school most of the time, while most serious problems at
school involving students are caused by the same small number of students who
violate rules and/or laws repeatedly with no intent of changing. Three, the students at school who do cooperate, who already excel at school, who could excel
at school, who could improve at school, who are willing to respond to efforts
made on their behalf, plus the adults at school deserve to work without their educational experiences or careers being limited, frequently interrupted, jeopard-
ized or threatened by criminal, semicriminal, destructive, or incorrigible students.
These same cooperative students and the adults at school deserve to have their
health and safety protected. A fifteen-year-old criminal's right to an education

does not have to mean going to a typical school where the rights of education and safety for other people have been or likely could be compromised.

Educating every student is important; however, educating every student in the entire range of circumstances that students bring to school with them now in one school building with one overall educational program and staff is unrealistic. No one company manufactures or sells every product in the marketplace. No one doctor treats every possible medical condition. No one meal served three times a day would meet all of the nutritional needs of every person every day for a life-time. No one exercise activity meets all of the health and fitness requirements for any person even if that activity is done correctly every day.

The goal of universal education for all students in the United States is a proper goal. The assumption that one school can meet all of the needs of all students to-day is faulty. Educational needs of all students can be met if many educational options, programs, and locations are used. For some, if not many or most, of the students in the other 5 to 10 percent, alternative educational programs provided at alternative locations are needed.

"But it is unfair to take those students out of their local school? Won't that just upset them?"

What is more unfair is to keep those students in a school where despite the end-less and heroic efforts by everyone involved to effectively educate the students, little or no progress is being made while continued crimes are being committed by the student, continued severe disruptions are being caused by the student, plus the safe and productive environment that everyone else needs to work in is being damaged.

Is it practical, reasonable, and efficient for every school to provide the full range of education, counseling, rehabilitation, psychological, physical health, mental health, family support, and other services needed by everyone in the school? No. There are practicality and efficiency benefits when certain educa-tional services are provided through specialized programs at exclusive locations to meet specialized needs.

"But how will decisions be made about which students attend alternative pro-grams? How can this be done fairly so people at schools don't just try to get rid of certain students they are tired of dealing with or whose family has been im-possible to work with?"

Alternative educational schools already exist, so procedures for placing stu-dents in those schools have been established. Experts in school law, school regu-lations, school policies, budgets, juvenile justice, and related issues will need to help answer questions in these areas. Some significant leadership and communi-cation efforts will be needed to build awareness of and support for expansion of alternative education. Governors, state commissioners of education, attorneys general of states, state legislators, school district superintendents, school board members, and community leaders will need to lead. For the goal of universal ed-ucation to be reached, the history in this country shows that the default delivery system traditionally has been one school that every student from a certain geographic district attends. However, the current reality is that the complexity of needs, circumstances, problems, syndromes, situations, conditions, habits, police records, and family difficulties usually cannot be resolved by the efforts that one school can make while it also provides proper educational services, opportunities, challenges, and experiences for students who respond well to a regular school program. When the range of students is from the criminal to the saint, from the destructive to the cooperative, from the incorrigible to the exemplary, from the mentally ill to the mentally healthy, from the students who repeatedly threaten the rights of other people to the students who repeatedly are ready, willing, able to do more and do better if criminals and incorrigibles were not disrupting the educational environment and process, it is essential that the current reality be acknowledged with a range of educational programs offered exclusively at specialized locations.

It can be helpful to personalize the concepts and the recommendations in this chapter. Three students who are in the other 5 to 10 percent will introduce themselves.

STUDENT 1

I'm Tony McKenzie. I'm fifteen years old and on the days I come to school I'm in the ninth grade. I'm absent a lot. I skip school a lot. School is stupid. I show up sometimes to see friends or keep out of court. There's some law about missing school. My mother had to go to court. So, I'll probably show up more, but who knows.

I did kind of like elementary school. Middle school was awful. I flunked sixth grade. Actually I flunked sixth grade twice. There I was as a thirteen-year-old in the sixth grade. Same teachers. Same stuff. I didn't care much. I got to school in time to eat breakfast. I could do that at home, but why bother if the school does it for you? I liked lunch because it was fun to talk to friends. I finally finished middle school. I did not learn anything. I spent a lot of time in programs or in groups that the counselor organized.

In the eighth grade I was in everything but class. I went to the anger management group and the social skills group and the grief recovery group. I made up reasons to go to some groups. I said my dog died and I was upset, plus I said my cousin was on drugs and was sick, so they let me go to grief recovery group. I never had a dog and my only cousin is some straight A student in another state. My mom signed the papers for me to attend the groups. I'd rather go to a dumb group meeting than a dumb class.

So I get to high school. It's worse than middle school. I'm in all of the slow and low classes except for algebra. My schedule had some problem so the only algebra class was with superbrains. I flunked most classes. It's funny. I made a 91 on an algebra test. Algebra is easy, it's just dumb. The teacher said, "See what you can do when you work." Fooled him. It was no work. It was seventh grade math all over again.

So in ninth grade our school starts this new program for sixteen-year-olds. They know we'll all drop out. Nobody stays in high school until they are twenty. The new program is so bad. I had to go because the judge said so. Yeah, I've got a police record. Shoplifting. Vandalism. I beat up a guy at school. Actually I did that to two different guys. They wouldn't give me money for lunch. I told them to pay or get hurt. They had plenty of money. The second time it was called assault. The school cop arrested me. The juvenile court sent me home with all kinds of warnings. The judge said I had to attend the Second Chance program at my school. Second Chance is a bunch of teenagers with police records. We meet once a week to eat pizza and tell lies about how we are going to do better.

I'll get a job after I drop out, but I think I'll finish ninth grade. Then I'll work at a car wash. Two hundred dollars a week sounds good. The guy who runs the car wash said I can work there. I'll wait until summer for good weather.

My Second Chance mentor told me that car wash jobs will be gone someday. Machines will wash cars. No big deal. I can take care of myself. There are other ways to make money. I do make money at school. About five or six scared ninth graders give me money so I don't beat them up. Even after I drop out I can come bother them and get more money.

I did think about playing football this year. I like the idea of smashing people on the other team. My grades were too low. Football might have been cool, but so what.

The best year was my second year in sixth grade. I knew exactly how to get kicked out of class. I'd say something to another student or I'd interrupt the teacher or I'd shoot a paper wad with a rubber band. I'm out of there. I'd sit in the office and then go to the in-school suspension room far away from teachers. I still got to eat lunch. I did the same thing over and over. I did get suspended a few times. Then I'd run around the neighborhood and tear stuff up. I got caught once or twice, but most times I never got caught.

The only plan I have is to get a car. I'll work at the car wash and get some money. I might even work at a car body shop. It's so easy to fix cars. Well, it's easy for me. My stepfather works on cars. He taught me how to do easy paint job repairs. People will pay $300 to get a small car swatch painted. If I can do one of those a week, I can buy a car. My school counselor said that when I'm a junior in high school I can go to car repair training. I ain't going to be no high school junior. Maybe if sixth grade had been car repair things would be different. But who cares. I know what I'm doing.

So, that's it. School is no good for me. It's almost time to quit. I'm getting ready to do that. But I need to get some more money from those scared ninth graders, so I'll stay for a few more weeks. It's easy money.

STUDENT 2

My name is, wait a minute, why am I telling you? I don't know you. You ain't my momma and you sure ain't my daddy, so don't tell me what to do. I do whatever I want to do.

Tiffany. Tiffany Anne Madison if you have to know it all. My mother named me for some actress or singer or something.

I'm in the seventh grade. Again. I'll probably pass this time. I haven't decided yet. Passing is easy. I just might not want to fool with it.

So, you want to ask me a bunch of questions so you can help me, right? Come on, man, I've heard it all before. Since you are new, I'll help you out. All you people from courts and agencies come visit the juvenile offenders in school like it's supposed to change anything. Get real. I know what you want to hear. I know your bluffs about having me arrested again. Let's just get this over with.

Yes, I've used drugs, alcohol, marijuana, and some other stuff. It's all dumb. I really think it's dumb. I listen to my friends when they are drunk or high. They sound so stupid. I just do it to get along with my friends. No, I don't want new friends.

Yes, I'm court involved. I've been arrested a few times for being disorderly and for tearing up property. I spent one night in juvenile detention. So what. Usually I just get sent home with my family. Then you come check on me or someone else does. Like I care.

School. I pretty much hate it. My friends and I take up for each other. The teachers are, well, I don't take them seriously. Everything we do is the same old stuff.

What am I good at? Not much. Well, two things. I'm an awesome skateboarder. I really am good at it. And, this sounds funny, but I can cook. Nobody else at my house can cook. I taught myself pretty much.

School. No, I already told you. It's dumb and boring. What a stupid place. Come on, they think I'll do better this year because I've already had all of this seventh grade stuff. It was dumb last year. It is dumb this year. Do you know anybody who did a lot better when they repeated a grade? I didn't think so.

What am I going to be when I grow up? Who says I'll grow up? Who says I'm not already grown up? Okay. I'll be a . . . I don't know, I'll be a cook at some restaurant. No, I'll own a restaurant. That's it. I'll own a restaurant that has all kinds of skateboard stuff. Pictures, video games, virtual skateboards, maybe even some skateboard equipment for sale. Maybe my restaurant could be right next to a skateboard park. I'll call the restaurant, maybe, I mean, Boarders, that's it. Boarders like skateboarders. So, that's what I'll do when I grow up. How about you? What are you going to do when you grow up and don't mess with thirteen-year-old skateboarders anymore? What's your real job going to be?

Do I date? Get real. Nobody dates. That was like fifty years ago. We all hang out together. My friends and I go places as a group. The girls think the boys are silly and the boys think the girls are gossips, but we all get along because nobody else likes us. We're the group that nobody else likes. We like that because we don't like anybody else.

School. I told you. It's dumb. Classes are the same old thing over and over. I flunked, but if I was in eighth grade it would be the same dull stuff over and over. Who cares? I didn't flunk because I'm stupid. I flunked because I'm smart enough to see how stupid all this is. Here's an example. The math teacher keeps talking about something called integers. Is that a real word? Can you explain what it means? No you can't. See how stupid it all is. I'm a great reader. Really, I can read anything. I flunked my English class last year because I never read the dumb stories. Who cares about some stupid short story from England a long time ago?

I'll probably get suspended from school today or tomorrow. This is Tuesday and I don't want to be here Thursday or Friday. Maybe I'll use some trash talk in class. That's usually good for a two-day suspension. It's worked before.

I might try to stay out of court. That was kind of a pain. The judge got all serious. I'm not scared of her or of jail, but it was weird when that door locked and I was trapped in my cell. They called it my room, like it has metal bars and a lock; it's a jail, not a room. But I can steal at school and never go to jail. It's easy. A crime at school almost never gets called a crime. Do the same stuff at a store and it's a crime. Easy system to beat.

That's about it. I just don't' have much use for school. I can't see how that could ever change.

STUDENT 3

I graduate from high school in two months. Our school had some essay contest for seniors. The topic was what high school has meant to us. That's easy. Nothing. Absolutely nothing. The school means nothing to me and I mean nothing to it.

Well, that last part may not be exactly right. I might mean something to the school. But it's not good. The teachers hate me. They really hate me. The principal and the assistant principals hate me. I get in trouble a lot, but it's never awful, serious, get arrested trouble. Fact is, I've never been arrested. I've been suspended from high school several times each year. Never more than eight or nine days in a year.

Here's what I think the teachers really hate. I've never done anything so bad that I could get kicked out of school. I get suspended and I come back. I get in trouble and my family has a conference with a school counselor and an assistant principal. Same old stuff.

One other thing. I never fail a class. No student is better at making D's than I am. I keep track of my grades. I know what I need to do to pass each class. I do just enough to make D grades. Sometimes I make a C grade but not on purpose. Some classes are just so easy.

I arrive late to classes a lot. The teachers hate it because it interrupts their work. Hey, I was talking to a friend. What's the hurry? I skip some classes. Sometimes I get caught. I skip a full day sometimes. I don't steal things or tear up the place. I do bother a lot of people. I like to attend meetings of clubs that I don't belong to just to bother them. I like to ask really off-the-wall questions in class. I like to put lots of trash talk in my homework papers just to see if the teacher really reads them.

I got in all kinds of trouble in middle school, but I never flunked a class. The principal would lecture me in her office about my childish actions. She'd check the computer screen to see my grades. I knew she hated it when the screen showed I passed everything. She could never tell me that my bad behavior would make me fail a year. I was bad because it was fun. School is boring. I needed some excitement.

High school was sort of different. The principal almost never met with me. An assistant principal did. I can hear them now. Steven Jefferson Middenton, he would say to get my attention, I guess. Nobody else ever calls me by my full name. I'd listen but never take it seriously. Eventually, if a teacher wrote a discipline report about me, the assistant principal would see me at lunch in the cafeteria and tell me the punishment. That saved him and me some time.

So, I'm a repeat offender, but misdemeanors only, no felonies. I show off in class or use nasty words on homework. I'm late to class or I skip class or I skip school. I do not come to class prepared. I don't study much. I pass and I get by. I'm a pain to teachers and some students, but they can't do anything serious to me. I know I've kept some other students from doing their best. I think one teacher quit because of me and my constant disruptions in her class. I know a few substitute teachers will not come to the school because of me.

But I'll graduate soon. The teachers will be thrilled. But there are other students like me. Some even have an excuse for their misbehavior because of some condition. I know those students. Some of them just use the so-called condition as an excuse. It's all pretty dumb. I hope whatever I do after high school is this easy to pass.

I do give the schools credit for trying. In elementary school there was some after school program I attended. It was supposed to teach me how to get along with other students. It did not work at all. Then there was some community mentor project where I went to a meeting at school every week to hear somebody talk about college and how important it was to plan ahead. I am not going to college. I never intended to. But that fifth grade mentor meeting got me out of classes.

That's when I started figuring out the system. I kept getting in little bits of trouble and I'd get sent to some meetings or some programs. Middle school had tons of those. I made sure I went to all of them and I made sure that nothing ever worked so I could go to more.

In high school I was told that I was at risk for failing and dropping out. No way. I knew how to pass a class. My mom promised me a car for the start of my senior year if I never failed a high school class. I kept the car as long as I kept passing. No F's on my report card. She said I was supposed to do better than just pass. That was not the deal and she knew it. My high school used a bunch of alternative discipline actions. My favorite was school service. I'll clean the cafeteria any time. It gets me out of class. So I'd disrupt a class I hated anyway and be given school service during that class time for a few days.

I've been a constant pain in the neck to people at school. I could have made much better grades, but what's the point? I could have behaved better, but why? I was determined to do it my way and nobody ever caught me doing anything awful. I caused more little problems than any student in history, but there was no limit on little problems like, five little problems in one month equals one big problem and three big problems in a year equals being sent to some really restrictive place. I think I beat the system. The system never did beat my methods.

There are statistics and estimates which show that about 5 percent of students in middle schools and high schools cause serious problems. The options available to resolve those problems need to be expanded. The current reality is that the category of misbehaviors at school includes criminal misconduct for which schools usually have no effective corrective action. When a student commits a crime at school, is suspended from school for five days or ten days, and then returns to the same school, is it reasonable to expect no further misconduct? If the misconduct was a crime, did the school authorities have efficient help and support from police and the juvenile justice system? If the student who committed the crime has a history of similar misbehavior, does it suggest that more of the same limited actions will not reverse the pattern, the habit, the likelihood of misbehavior? To resolve these issues that may confront principals, assistant principals, and school counselors continuously, it is important to have alternatives that in earlier decades might not have been needed. For the rehabilitation of the juvenile offender and for the health, safety, and education of other students and adults at school, realistic alternatives are needed.

For the next 5 percent of students whose chronic, continued, intentional, incorrigible misconduct at school is not criminal but is disruptive and destructive, who resist all efforts that educators at a regular school can make, assignment to an alternative educational placement program and setting is more important than ever. The student in question needs a different educational experience. The other students and the educators at the school need to be allowed to direct their attention to their work without the continuous disorder caused by the incorrigibles.

The rise in the number of students who are criminal, semicriminal, habitually destructive or disorderly, chronically incorrigible has not been matched with an equal increase in a willingness to deal directly with these students or with an increase in the options available for dealing with these students. The same rise in the number of students who are criminal, semicriminal, habitually destructive or disorderly, chronically incorrigible has not been matched with an equal increase in concern for the health, safety, and work environment of the students who cooperate and the adults who work at school.

The other 5 to 10 percent of students can be effectively educated and/or rehabilitated if the right decisions are made for placement in an educational juvenile justice rehabilitation facility. Some of the other 5 to 10 percent of students might straighten up if they realized that decisions can be imposed on them. Families of some of the other 5 to 10 percent of students might become more concerned and involved if they knew that educational decisions can be imposed on them.

Ask educators whose careers span the past two or three decades about the trends and the students mentioned in this chapter. "Oh, yes, things are different. But what can we do? Our hands are tied. Families threaten to sue even when their child caused the problem. The central office people don't work at schools, so they think we can handle anything. Politicians pass these impossible laws and expect us to make them work. Give one of those politicians a week in my classroom and they'll cry for help as they run out the door on the first day." Since teachers are asked to deal with problems and situations that did not exist decades ago in the severity, numbers, or frequency that now exist, innovative options are needed.

"It's the same students, over and over. The same ones get in trouble. The same ones make low grades. No matter what we do, the same students cause most of the problems." That frustration, disappointment, and confusion has been commonly expressed by teachers I have known from many different schools in many different school districts. Perhaps 90 percent of the serious misbehaviors are caused by 10 percent of the students. Perhaps 90 percent of the serious academic failures or very low performing results are from 10 percent of the students. Those two 10 percent groups probably have much overlap as students with severe and repeated misbehavior problems may be most likely to have severe and repeated academic problems.

When month after month and year after year the same students are causing most of the discipline problems and are having many of the academic problems, it is reasonable to consider an alternative to what has not worked. When the regular school program is not working despite all efforts and variations, perhaps the only option is an alternative program and location. Why stay at the same place, keep causing problems, and keep failing when another approach at another place could provide unique opportunities and options?

It's as if a doctor said to a patient, "We have some very good nurses in this office and we have some very good equipment. We'll do all we can for you with what we have. Of course, if you went to a specialist or a hospital, they could do more. And if you had followed all the advice I've given you through the years, you would be better off. But we'll do all we can. I'm your family doctor and this office is convenient for you."

That medical approach would be unacceptable and unethical. But that approach is what educators are sometimes forced to do when no alternatives exist or when a student and/or the student's family can refuse to take advantage of the available alternatives. The creation of and the assignment to attend alternative educational programs may have costs, complexities, and controversies; however, ignoring the need for these alternatives is more costly. Lawmakers, policy makers, regulation writers, elected public officials, school superintendents, and other people in leadership or management positions need to take responsibility for these very necessary changes. To delay action is to unnecessarily permit serious problems to become severe critical conditions.

Most students at most schools are doing what they are supposed to be doing most of the time. They can become extreme students. They can become more challenged, more fascinated, more successful if they are already extreme students. For the benefit of these students who can do well in a regular school setting and for the benefit of the other 5 to 10 percent who cannot or will not do well in a regular school setting, more aggressive leadership on and actions with alternative education are needed now.

The next chapter is written for and about students, although adults are welcome to read it and share it with students. The chapter is for and about students who are already in the extreme student category and who need nurturing, development, encouragement, or recognition. It is also for and about students who are not yet in the extreme category but can and should become extreme students.

Chapter 8

School Thoughts: About, For, and Inspired by Extreme Students

There are issues of radical importance that emerge from the classrooms, hallways, cafeterias, and offices of schools. There are concerns of radical importance that linger in the hearts, minds, and souls of teachers, students, and school administrators. There are mistakes made and goals reached within our schools. There are political battles about education fought so far away from schools that the combatants should be required to declare a truce, come substitute teach for a month, and encounter reality for the first time.

The school thoughts that follow raise questions, concerns, issues, ideas, hopes, and answers. This chapter is not intended to be a pep rally. It is intended to provoke thinking and arouse action, which means it is designed to cause learning that causes more learning.

These thirty-one school thoughts can be read individually, a few at a time, or as a chapter. There are thirty-one school thoughts, so you can read one school thought each day during a month and repeat that process the next month.

SCHOOL THOUGHT 1

Please think like I think. Not all of the time. You have to act like an adult and you have to be a grown-up, but every now and then, just think like I think.

I think that school is so boring, very boring, seriously boring, make-me-fall-asleep boring. Elementary school was okay until the fifth grade. For some reason that year was just one big review. It was awful. We did the same old stuff from third grade and fourth grade. My guess is that the teacher just made it easy on herself and on us. I liked it being easy and stuff, but, you know, even easy got old. I'm not asking for work, just for something interesting.

So, think like I think. I'm thirteen years old and in the eighth grade. I make okay grades, mostly C's and some B's. I do make A's in band because I'm good at trumpet. I like trumpet. I even played the national anthem once at a college football game. Did you know that? Did you ever ask me about that? It was on TV and everything. If you could think like me you'd know how really cool and really nervous it was to be in front of that crowd. I also play trumpet at my church sometimes and at Christmas I play for old people at a nursing home. Have you ever done anything like that?

I think about high school. I'm kind of scared, but marching band sounds neat. My big sister is in marching band. She says it's the most fun part of high school because they go on a lot of trips.

Think like me sometimes. My parents got divorced two years ago. I hated it. I hated everything. I did really bad in school after that. I finally quit hating life, but it's still a pain. Birthdays are strange because I don't see my dad because he moved away. We had to sell our old house that I really liked. So whenever you talk about taking something home to your parents, I get mad because I can't take something home to my parents.

Teachers always tell me I'm not working up to my potential. As if I didn't already know. I could probably make better grades, but come on, it's just middle school. I'll do better in high school. If I could take band all day now I'd do great. If you really want me to reach my potential, then just let me play trumpet all day or do something with music all day. That would be so cool. I really would work hard on that.

SCHOOL THOUGHT 2

High school has been great. The teachers have encouraged me and challenged me. My coaches have pushed me hard in soccer and track. When our girl's soccer team won the regional tournament last October it was the best feeling ever, well almost.

The truth is, as much as I like soccer, I like science more and I like using computers in science more than soccer or track put together. It all began when I was in ninth grade and the school had that student-to-student deal. It was all set up by computer. Ninth grade girls got a student mentor who was a junior or senior girl. The same plan was set up for boys. My mentor was the ultimate brain. She knew more science than college professors. She always won science competitions. She earned a full scholarship to the best known colleges in the country and some state schools. She got me interested in science.

Well, I had to do a science project and I decided to study the impact of proper hydration on athletes. I researched track runners, not sprinters, but distance runners who competed in the two-mile run. How did drinking the proper fluids, in the proper amount, and at the right time, help them? Each year in high school I took that project to a deeper level. I'm almost an expert on the subject now. I got some scholarship offers from companies and scientist groups. They seem really interested in my research.

My senior year community service project was to go to some middle schools and show students how cool science is when you use science in sports. I wish somebody had told me that when I was in middle school.

I'll study sports medicine and sports marketing in college. I'll invent some new athletic training hydration products and techniques. Be sure to buy stock in my company when we go public. I hope my teachers and my mentor invest in the company. They deserve the big money we will make.

SCHOOL THOUGHT 3

"What can I do? We took away everything. He has no phone, no TV, no computer, and no music. He still makes bad grades. He still gets in trouble. What can we do?"

"What's he interested in? What good hobbies or interests does he have?"

The mother smiled, paused, and spoke in a subdued tone. "It's funny to think about that. In elementary school he was interested in animals. He read, he asked questions, he went to the zoo, he read more. He was crazy about animals. Even in middle school he kept reading about animals. He took care of every pet in the neighborhood."

"Is he still interested in animals?" the hopeful teacher asked.

"He might be. My mother just got a dog to keep her company and for safety. Shawn asked if he could go see Nana and the dog. But he's grounded because of all the school stuff, getting in trouble and bad grades."

The teacher wondered, "Does Shawn know that our high school has a partnership with some farmers? Some juniors go out to farms that have been in families for generations to learn about local history and to learn how modern farming is done. Maybe Shawn could go to that farm one day. It might get him interested in school again."

It might help make Shawn an extreme student.

SCHOOL THOUGHT 4

I think it was in the sixth grade or maybe the seventh grade. Everything fell apart. I had to go to a different school than all of my friends because of the dumb, what's it called? Oh yeah, redistricting. There I was alone at some middle school. I hated it. My grades were bad for the first time ever. I didn't care. My teachers were, you know, they were teachers. They made us read and take tests. One teacher showed videos all the time. That was easy, but videos can get boring after a few months.

It may sound funny, but I loved eighth grade. I got picked to be in some new job training program. I got to leave that dumb school and go to the Technical Occupational Opportunity Leadership School. The nickname was TOOLS. They said we were being given this once in a lifetime opportunity to learn how to do really neat jobs like put computers together and repair cars and build houses. I loved it. I worked hard. Math for building a house was worth doing. So was everything else.

So, here I am a junior in high school. I'm in my fourth year of the TOOLS program. I've taken all the required classes for graduation each year, but it was with what my teachers called hammer and nails instead of textbooks and worksheets. I had to read, but it was real stuff not stories nobody cares about and nobody can understand.

Get this. I've learned some Japanese. It helps me when I visit job sites that are owned by Japanese companies. Tell my sixth grade teachers that I learned Japanese and they will not believe you.

I like school. I work hard. I ask a lot of questions. I read a lot. I think a lot, I really concentrate on what I'm doing. I know some students who dropped out, but if they had been in TOOLS they would still be here. Our slogan is "Just Give Me the TOOLS." That's me. Someday you'll pay me a lot of money to build your house.

SCHOOL THOUGHT 5

After ten years of teaching I asked myself if I could continue or not. Something about this just is not working. I can't put in more hours. My children need me when they get home from their school. My husband and I need more time to be together. My aunt needs help with day-to-day chores. Don't get me wrong. I want to keep teaching. My principal tells me I'm a great teacher. I tell him I'm a very tired, very frustrated, and very uncertain about the future teacher.

Here's my disappointment. Bless their hearts; most of my ninth graders are good people who cooperate and work. But in every class, there are three or four or five who obviously do not care about school. They destroy everything for everyone else. Why are they allowed to keep coming to school and bothering everyone?

I know my best students could do even better work if I could give them the time I lose trying to control the "can't wait to dropout" group. My average students really could excel with more guidance from me, but guess what? The young criminals steal our class time with their disruptions. Sure, they get disciplined, but it means nothing to them and it does nothing to them.

So, I need some help. I need someone who makes the big money and has the big power to realize what we are dealing with and give us some options. I'm sure those five students who disrupt my class cause problems in other classes. I really believe that those same five students can learn and can succeed in school, but in a program just for them. There they learn more and do better while the other students who are no longer bothered, bullied, teased, stolen from, threatened, extorted, intimidated, hit, or just interrupted in class could really thrive.

It's time that the students who work, behave, and cooperate be given what they deserve without having their education limited by time lost due to the juvenile offenders. Creating the laws and policies to make that happen could put some politician in the history books.

SCHOOL THOUGHT 6

They make my day. Without intending to, without trying to, without being obligated to, without any extraordinary effort, they make my day.

It is not their job to make my day. It is their job to make their day, to be the best possible high school students they can be every day. They do their job with exemplary manners, skill, honor, greatness, and dedication.

I wish I had their wisdom, vibrant personalities, wit, charm, ability, future, dispositions, poise, social grace, brainpower, when I was a high school junior. It is not their youth I wish for. It is their integrity, their eagerness to get the most out of life, their common sense, their uncommon brilliance, their most likely to live a completely wonderful life destiny.

They make my day. Four high school students who smile when they see me, talk politely with me, honestly share ideas and convictions, give me a reality check about teaching and give me hope that educators still touch lives. They touch my life in ways that I could not expect but can only give thanks for. They even remind me that despite my abandoned dreams and missed opportunities, despite my teenage failures and adult disappointments, school can still be a place where teachers can create and develop extreme students who, without intending to, teach their teachers.

I cannot be seventeen again. I would dearly love to be a teenager again, but only in my dreams is that possible. Or is there a way? I cannot become seventeen, but I can share the experience that students have as they are seventeen. I can contribute to their seventeenness. Then, when they move on, a new group of first-time seventeen-year-olds enters the classroom. I cannot be seventeen again, but I can help make each seventeen-year-old's once in a lifetime experience of being seventeen the best possible experience. I'm a teacher so that's what I get to do.

SCHOOL THOUGHT 7

Each school can create an idea factory. The e-mail system to communicate the ideas is available. Trading ideas will create, inspire, and produce new ideas. That is what idea factories do.

How does it work? Very, very easily. Teachers create lesson plans and teaching activities using their word processing function on their computer at school or elsewhere. The lesson plans and teaching activities are saved on the computer and then are e-mailed to the faculty of the school or to an idea factory electronic address that everyone can access.

There are many hours invested each week by teachers as they design lesson plans and teaching activities. Teachers in the same school rarely get to observe one another. Time in the typical school day for teachers to meet and trade ideas is limited. The electronic method of trading ideas eliminates the limits of time and location.

Please note, when Teacher A uses an idea from Teacher B, some changes will be needed because Teacher A's students bring a unique collection of life experiences, knowledge, interests, and talents. The idea factory helps communicate ideas which then inspire the creation of more ideas.

SCHOOL THOUGHT 8

Life is not paint by numbers, fill in the blank, multiple choice, true–false, or prepackaged. Students are not lowest common denominator, generic, prepackaged, or identical. Teachers also have individuality. So why impose a limited, predictable, confined set of prefabricated tasks—read the textbook, answer the questions at the end of the chapter, take the publisher-provided test on Friday, vibrantly live real life on the weekend, and then start the same numbing process on Monday with the next chapter?

SCHOOL THOUGHT 9

The biggest rewards and celebrations in many middle schools and high schools are for athletic achievement. Does that make sense? What message does that communicate?

Athletic teams work hard and earn recognition. Athletic celebrations are beneficial parts of the school culture, school traditions, the school community, and the teenage years.

The concern is that when schools have frequent, elaborate, and visible celebrations of athletic achievement, the message sent is that making a game-winning three-point shot in basketball is more important than making a top-rated science fair project. The message sent by giving parades and rings to students who carry a football into the end zone while doing very little for students who consistently carry books home to study, make honor roll grades, and earn superior test scores is that football points matter more than grade point averages.

The recommendation is to celebrate and reward academic progress and academic achievement more publicly, more enthusiastically, and more generously than athletic success is celebrated. Notice what is done for athletic rewards and always ask, Are we doing more to encourage, celebrate, and reward students as students than we do for students as athletes?

SCHOOL THOUGHT 10

There are many answers to the questions from a parent or guardian of a student whose academic and/or behavior results at school are bad. One answer is, "Show up. Come to school. Go to classes with your child. Come back in a few days. Come back again after that on an unpredictable schedule. The son or daughter needs to know that you take school seriously enough to be there." Some parents and guardians of middle school students attend sixth grade orientation the week before school begins and are never seen again until a ceremony is held to honor eighth graders three years later. What message does that send to a thirteen-year-old? "But it would embarrass my child if I came to school." Does it embarrass your child when you cheer for him at a baseball game, attend her music recital, or go to summer camp for a family day? Whether spoken or not, the child realizes by your presence and your time that you care enough to be there.

"But my child makes great grades and never gets in trouble. Why should I visit her class?" To see her success. To see the school experiences she has and build on them. "That math you did in class today is just like what the accountant for our company does. Here, I'll show you how it works."

Are high school students too old and too sophisticated to benefit from parent/guardian involvement at school? Of course not. Many parents and guardians spend many hours helping with high school athletic events, marching band competitions, or other extracurricular activities. Similar support for and involvement in academic work at school can be done.

Why would a parent or guardian act in ways that send this message to a fourteen-year-old high school freshman: "I'm going to be very aware of everything you do, except for school. You go to school for the next four years and I'll attend your graduation. Everything else in your life I will be aware of and sometimes involved in, but you do school on your own."

SCHOOL THOUGHT 11

How do teachers cause learning that causes more learning to be sought and obtained? What does that mean? What can teachers do to teach so that two goals are reached: (1) learning is caused and (2) the experience the students have that caused the intended learning also intrigued, fascinated, amazed, and motivated students to eagerly seek more learning.

One way is to begin with the perspective that what is done in the classroom is not finite. "Today we will learn about the geography of Alaska." Okay, that could include facts, statistics, pictures, stories, skits, compare and contrast, websites, a two-minute virtual trip to Alaska via edited video, or an Alaska-cam Internet journey. If the classroom activity is limited to pages 65–68 of the geography textbook and two sets of questions in the book, the learning is finite. If the activities include the book and several other ways of learning, the results can include (1) meaningful learning was caused and (2) an interest in learning more was inspired. Why be concerned with causing learning that causes more learning? What's your answer to that question?

SCHOOL THOUGHT 12

Alternative schools sometimes have a reputation as boot camps where the only purpose is to reform juvenile criminals. Reality is that the teenage population, and some people in younger groups than that, includes some criminals who need to be reformed, rehabilitated, and educated in severely restrictive alternative schools. Some of those schools need to become joint ventures of the juvenile justice system, the police department, and the court system so movement in the community is monitored, restricted, or eliminated as needed.

There are other concepts of alternative schools that merit increased attention. Some middle school students have internally dropped out of school. They arrive at school, eat breakfast and lunch, disrupt classes, bully students, steal and/or fight. They get suspended from school and return to once again eat two meals, bother people, and steal or fight. They have no intention of doing anything productive at school; however, on weekends they actually get something done. They work on a car. They fix a bicycle. They help an uncle drywall the basement of a house he recently bought and is fixing up. How could school get the attention and the commitment of these students?

One idea is the old-fashioned shop class or industrial arts class, as it was later known. Students in those classes built furniture, wired lamps, designed projects using drafting skills, and invented new projects to complete. Those were problem-solving, multiple intelligence classes before those approaches to teaching had formal names and active advocates.

"But shop class is outdated. And it sounds like it prepares you only for a certain job." Okay, update it, give it a new name if necessary, and expand the job preparations. From carpentry to electrical work, from welding to car repair, from heating/ventilation/air-conditioning work to computer repair, from web design to video or audio broadcasting, the hands-on and brains-on activities that these experiences can provide could build new commitment from middle school or high school students who are already resisting school and could be another way to create, nurture, guide, inspire, and challenge extreme students.

In the well-intentioned, honorable effort to increase the academic achievement of every student, it is not necessary to limit the approaches used to traditional college preparation education. For some students, endless academic achievements can come through thinking about how to build a piece of furniture, designing the furniture, reading, calculating, building, correcting, rebuilding, and then selling the furniture.

"But is building furniture a job for the future?" Well, will people in the future still buy furniture? "What if future furniture is built by robots?" Include robotics in the experience the middle school and high school students have in their new, improved, modern, twenty-first century shop/industrial arts/vocational/technical/career alternative school.

SCHOOL THOUGHT 13

"They'll be fine. They are gifted and talented. They'll make all A's. They can do it all on their own."

An easy A grade suggests that the student mastered the requirements with minimal or moderate effort. The student does geometric proofs with amazing ease. Geometry just comes easily to the student. The goal is not to impose brutally hard demands on this student. Rather, the goal is to build on this success in geometry and provide a learning challenge for the student so academic growth occurs. What happens if the student is given the opportunity to read some of the original writings of Euclid from around 300 BC to experience some of the original concepts of geometry? That could be an academic challenge that enables the student to advance from making an easy A grade to earning a difficult A through an interesting intellectual endeavor that stretches his or her mind and expands learning.

The best students can become bored at school because "everything is so easy, it's the same stuff over and over." The best students deserve the academic experience that most effectively nurtures and challenges them just as the student who has difficulty learning or refuses to learn, needs experiences that most effectively cause them to learn.

SCHOOL THOUGHT 14

"How can I really be the type of teacher who always fully nurtures the wholesome intellectual curiosity for knowledge within students?"

Live that way yourself. Be a person who in school and out of school fully explores, creates, nurtures, expands, and experiences your own wholesome intellectual curiosities for knowledge. Develop, nurture, guide, and challenge your own wholesome intellectual curiosities for knowledge about teaching, learning, students, hobbies, interests, talents, and skills. Identify new learning you would like to experience and become an extreme student of that topic. Teachers who develop extreme students are themselves extreme students of students, of teaching, of learning, of life.

SCHOOL THOUGHT 15

I am an extreme student, so in many ways, I am my brain and my mind. What my brain and my mind think, decide, become, know or do not think, decide, become, know is what I am.

Questions. Curiosities. Intellectual ambition. Academic hunger and thirst. Bold thoughts. Original ideas. Original ideas about old ideas. Unique insights. Mental confidence, preparation, resources, and courage to challenge the common, the superficial, the ordinary, the imposed limits, or the existing boundaries. The relentless effort to know more, understand deeply, question precisely, explore the mind's frontiers, and explore the infinity of thought. To combine a vibrant search for truth with a determined and orderly and structured, yet not totally predictable, approach. To thirst for real thinking. To find meaning, purpose, and reward in the search for knowledge and wisdom. To realize that there is no limit to thinking, to thought. To learn, learn more, and keep learning, forever, till death do us part. To live a life of wholesome intellectual curiosities for knowledge. This is to be an extreme student, now and forever.

SCHOOL THOUGHT 16

It is difficult to be a successful student if you are concerned about your health and safety at school. If you hear rumors of someone bringing a weapon to school it is difficult to concentrate fully on math, science, social studies, language arts, or other subjects. If other students tease you, pick on you, extort lunch money from you, steal, fight, disrupt, and destroy, it is hard to think or learn in that environment.

Are schools using every available method to increase safety? Are surveillance cameras placed throughout the school with the same thoroughness and sophistication as would be seen in a shopping mall or large department store? If stores use this method to protect merchandise, why are schools reluctant to use surveillance cameras to protect students, faculty, staff, and visitors?

What is done about students who repeatedly pick on, tease, bother, extort from, or steal from other students? Why are their rights to return to the same school after repeated misbehaviors and repeated discipline actions given more weight than the rights of other students to be safe, to be secure, to be left alone, to learn?

SCHOOL THOUGHT 17

Advice to high school students from several current and very successful high school students:

- Do not procrastinate.
- Do not fight.
- Do not argue with your teachers.
- Do not miss any school.
- Do not be an outsider—it is better to have friends because then you fit in and feel comfortable at school.
- Do not think that because you get good grades you are not cool. Too many students in high school worry about that A and think they will not be popular if they are smart.
- Learn to juggle school, work, free time, and other activities.
- Do not get behind in any subject, because with all of the work and fast pace it is extremely hard to catch up. Everything in high school builds on itself.
- Complete all work.
- Take advanced placement classes to further your collegiate opportunities.

SCHOOL THOUGHT 18

Advice from high school students for middle school students based on their reflections and lessons learned:

- Do all of your work.
- Do not fight.
- Learn as much as you can while you are there.
- Do not goof around.
- Make friends.
- If you do all of your work, you will succeed.
- Make sure you know what is going on in all of your math classes.
- Make sure your classes are advanced.

SCHOOL THOUGHT 19

The same high school students were asked for their reflections about elementary school. The passage of time did not keep strong memories from emerging.

- Show up and be a good student.
- Do not get into fights.

- Behave correctly.
- If you are a good reader you will do fine.
- Learn stuff.
- The best readers always did the best.
- When the students learned to read earlier in their career, it made their work a lot easier.
- As long as you actually do the work it becomes easier.

SCHOOL THOUGHT 20

When those high school students were asked what ideas or opinions they would like to offer to teachers, they provided these thoughts:

- Give us extra credit work and be sure it is enough to be worth doing.
- Let us earn free time in the classroom to talk with friends, even just one or two minutes.
- Let us earn a homework pass so there is one assignment we do not have to do.
- Give us more hands-on activities.
- Let us do more with art and drawing.
- When we have projects to do, give us choices so we can pick one we like and we don't feel like we have to do one thing.
- Make class so we want to be in it.
- Don't just give us book work to do.
- Be involved in class with us.
- If you just assign us book work there will be a lot of words that don't get read and we'll take a lot of quizzes with questions we can't answer.

SCHOOL THOUGHT 21

When asked to advise high school students on what not to do, the high school scholars I asked had these ideas:

- Do not sleep in class.
- Do not act out in class.
- Do not have distractions like magazines or cell phones.
- Do not take just the easiest classes.
- Do not avoid advanced classes.
- Don't take classes just because your friends are taking them.
- Do not disrupt other people.
- Do not blow off homework.

- Do not stress out over school; just do the work and manage things.
- Don't worry about next week; get your work for today done.

SCHOOL THOUGHT 22

It had been an absolutely awful, terrible, brutal, exhausting day at school. The power to arrest is not one of my options, but the two belligerent students in the cafeteria were a clear and present danger to the other two hundred students in that large room where escalation can be fast and chaotic. Stepping between the two foul-mouthed, thoughtless students became my duty. They backed down as my pulse raced up.

The two young thieves who stole a cell phone wasted an hour of my time as they lied and lied only to trap themselves in deception. Do the taxpayers know that such time is wasted in schools?

The student whose vulgar language in front of his father, two teachers, and me had to be suspended from school despite our efforts to provide other options.

The Academic Team match after school was on my schedule. Those young scholars who also behave perfectly deserve my support and appreciation. I took my weary body to the Academic Team match and I was quickly revitalized.

In truth, much of what I had to do today was unpleasant and troubling and was not related to education; rather, it was law enforcement, crisis management, and crowd control. Surveillance cameras throughout the building, a police officer, support staff to supervise the cafeteria, metal detectors at the entrances, and other resources could have helped me be an educator instead of a police officer. Will it change very much, very soon? Will we staff and equip schools for the realities of today? Unlikely. So, why endure?

One reason—extreme students. The students who are already extreme deserve encouragement, nurturing, growth experiences, challenges, and rewards. The students who are not yet extreme students need to be shown how and why becoming an extreme student should be their immediate goal.

To help make that happen, I must be where the students are. I must be at school. I must be an extreme teacher. I must be an extreme student of extreme students. I must acquire and cause extreme learning.

Easy? No. Worth it? Yes. It is who I am and it is what I do. When teaching chose me and when I chose teaching it must have been for better or worse, but with the enduring hope and with the real possibility that better will prevail.

SCHOOL THOUGHT 23

Extreme students know the importance of academic achievement. They also know the benefits of playing a sport, playing a musical instrument, being in a club, doing volunteer work in the community, accepting responsibilities in their family, getting exercise, eating healthy food, managing time, and sleeping sufficiently. Extreme does not mean obsessed. Extreme does not mean unbalanced. Extreme means the most, the best, the real, the pursuit of greatness, and the inspiring conviction that tomorrow can be even better than a great today.

SCHOOL THOUGHT 24

When eighth grade students were asked to think about what activity, method, discussion, or other event in this class has best helped them learn, their replies confirmed that great teachers use a variety of teaching methods and activities.

- "What really helps me learn in this class is when we have class discussion. I like hearing questions from all of my classmates and learning what answers we discuss."
- "Question-and-answer sessions. You would give us a topic of discussion and then students would ask questions that I wouldn't have thought of or had the answer to."
- "The projects, because I can be very creative sometimes."
- "When we made note cards. I remember the vocabulary words a whole lot better when I made cards for each of them"
- "The e-mails and Internet search about careers."
- "When we each got to use $100,000 to buy stocks helped me understand the stock market."
- "I liked making products like the milk store because it gave me a chance to use my imagination. I loved doing the hands-on learning."
- "How we did some projects in groups. I learned working with other people."

From a method as traditional as vocabulary flash cards to a method as new as the Internet to e-mail career questions to people currently working in those jobs, the students confirmed the benefit of a variety of activities. From a seminar discussion to creating a new business (the milk store we created did with milk what Starbucks has done with coffee), the students learned. Every student learned from each activity although each student had their preferred way of learning. Their curiosities were explored. Their questions were answered and were the basis for more questions. Those extreme students continue to discuss our class months after the class ended. What does that tell you?

SCHOOL THOUGHT 25

"My dad said you told him that I could get a letter of recommendation for college from you. I really appreciate that." The high school senior's voice mail message for me confirmed a conversation I had recently with his father. I knew the student during his three years of middle school. I returned his call later in the afternoon hoping that if the call were to a cell phone it would not ring during a class and get both of us in trouble. How would I explain to his teacher that I was disrupting the class?

We talked for a few minutes. He needed the letter quickly. His high school schedule included a community activity he would go to soon. I had reached him on his cell phone as he got in his car to leave his high school. He said he could come to our school now when I said the letter could be ready in fifteen minutes.

He very politely entered our school, the front office, and then my office. We corrected one part of the letter, printed it, and my promise was kept. He updated me on his college and career goals. He will do very well. Some parts of school have been a chore for him. His thinking and creativity go far beyond textbooks and worksheets. He will thrive on his chosen college campus where the creative arts are nourished.

He sent me a formal, proper thank-you note in the mail. It was an old-fashioned, pen and note card, postage stamp, and mailbox thank-you note. The note was appreciated. The visit with the student was even more appreciated. The opportunity to be of help was a joy. It is what we do. It is who we are.

SCHOOL THOUGHT 26

The student's father and mother never married each other. The student had not seen his father in years because that man was in jail. The student was often in trouble at school. The student never accepted responsibility for his misbehavior. Excuses were endless. His mother would occasionally come to school to offer new excuses and begin a new battle. The father reentered the picture once, made vast promises of how involved he intended to be, and then disappeared.

The parents were getting divorced and their children were distraught. "I can't help it. I hate school. This stupid divorce is ruining everything." The child spoke of the divorce as if it were an act of terrorism. To the child it was family terrorism. The child's description of divorce was similar to historians describing acts of war, invasions, battlefield encounters. As war causes casualties, it was obvious that this child was a casualty of divorce. A year later and the child was still suffering the anguish, confusion, emotional turmoil, and awkwardness of the aftermath of divorce.

The parent had given up completely. The father had not been involved in the lives of the children for years. The mother apparently tried now and then to be a parent, but boyfriends, alcohol, second- or third-shift jobs communicated to the children that they were on their own. The grandparents had taken the children for a few months, but the task was beyond their health, their age, their knowledge of this generation, and their energy level. It was all they could do to provide food, clothing, shelter, and some supervision. Social service agencies intervened and removed the children from the home. How does a child or a teenager concentrate on math and reading when his family falls apart?

Phone calls to the family were never returned. Letters were never acknowledged. E-mails were ignored. No emergency contact names or phone numbers were provided. A visit to the home brought this reply: "I know he's awful. He's like that at home. I can't do anything about it." The son had long since realized that his mother had given up on any effort to control him. She promised to come to school once to work out something. She came to school and was verbally abusive to every adult she encountered. She was told to leave the building. She left screaming.

The father came to school and explained the repeated efforts made by mental health experts to resolve his son's psychological disorders and syndromes. The twelve-year-old took a pharmacy of "medications," which, the father explained, never really solved the problems. What did the parent think that a school could do to help a twelve-year-old who was beyond the ability of physicians, psychologists, psychiatrists, and a mental health facility he had been in four times? The father was searching for help. Can society realistically expect a school to resolve every issue that impacts people between the ages of five and eighteen just because during those years people go to school? Schools educate. Schools are places of education. To assume that education can resolve every difficulty facing every child and teenager is unrealistic. To assume that a school can become a full-service social agency that corrects every family or personal issue impacting children and teenagers is to impose on schools what schools are not and should be designed to do.

The fifteen-year-old was seriously court involved. Repeated crimes in the community over several years had been prosecuted. The original wrist slaps by a court had become wrists enclosed in handcuffs and a fifteen-year-old locked up in the juvenile detention facility. Today that fifteen-year-old, still a criminal only more street shrewd than ever, returns to school with 1,800 students and 120 adults who present to her a group of easy victims for the next theft, the next extortion, the next threat, the next assault. The parents are apologetic for her illegal actions in the community and at school, but insist that she deserves to be at school. Who insists that the other 1,920 people at school deserve to be safe?

Families face difficulties sometimes through no fault of their own or through the fault of one disruptive family member. Families sometimes impose difficulties on their children and then expect the school to fix everything. When families cooperate with schools the results are more harmonious and productive. When families do their best to function as loving, caring, supporting, responsible groups, their children can have better experiences at school because they are having such wholesome experiences at home. When families are communicative with, involved at, and cooperative with schools, the results improve for their children.

Parents and guardians, please do everything properly possible to avoid the family struggles, complications, difficulties, dysfunctions, and divisions that make growing up healthy in heart, mind, body, and soul so challenging for children and teenagers. Parents and guardians, please avoid the actions or inactions that you know are harmful to ideal growth and development of children and teenagers. Harmony in your home will help create success for your child or teenager at school.

SCHOOL THOUGHT 27

The addition of games, group activities, computer applications, or other excitement-building classroom events should not be confused with assurance that the quality and/or quantity of learning will increase. High energy and high technology do not guarantee high student achievement. Learning activities must be designed as if the intent is educational engineering that is as specific in matching learning objective with classroom activities as an engineer's plans and designs for a bridge are matched with the subsequent construction process.

Identify the precise learning objective. Create the classroom activity that most effectively causes mastery of the learning objective by all students. Assess often to confirm learning to adjust your method of instruction. Use the learning activities that get the intended results.

SCHOOL THOUGHT 28

Plato makes sense. His ideas from ancient Greece are still profound, important, and useful. Beethoven's music is still unsurpassed. A century from now music that is temporarily popular for a few months today will have been forgotten if not deleted from musical memories. One hundred years from now Beethoven's masterpieces will still be heard as inspiring reminders of the possibility of perfection. The Founding Fathers of the United States collected and created superior political ideas and actions, structures and processes that continue to work despite societal changes.

Being up-to-date in school does not require abandoning all of the past in curriculum or instructional methods if what has stood the test of time can still help cause the intended learning today. Flash cards made of construction paper and crayon writing can help students today learn new vocabulary. Computer software can help students learn new vocabulary. Do what works with attention to results, not to when the teaching method or materials was invented.

SCHOOL THOUGHT 29

There are times when the classroom should be absolutely silent, calm, and reflective. This is silent indoor thinking time, or SIT, as my students prefer. We sit, read, write, think, and then we intellectually interact, we learn through listening, we reason and respond, we stretch our minds into new concepts, ideas, conclusions, and questions. Amid the busy-ness of the school day and amid the electrifying energy of children or teenagers, it is useful and beneficial to be still occasionally, to read silently, ponder deeply, and write purposefully. Vibrant interaction can, will, and should follow such contemplation.

SCHOOL THOUGHT 30

Education is more about needs than wants; however, using the wanted to help achieve the needed is practical, prudent, and productive. The student who wants to play basketball above all other possibilities can do math using basketball game statistics, can read stories with a basketball theme, can research the history of basketball, can analyze the economics of a sports arena, can evaluate the laws of science as they apply to a basketball in flight, can learn many parts of the curriculum through connections with basketball. For some students who have little or just not enough "want to" toward learning, some connections with their wholesome "want to" interests, knowledge, and talents can help increase mastery of the curriculum they need to know.

SCHOOL THOUGHT 31

Some students know what they like to learn about, but because of their life experience, which is limited to five years or up to eighteen and nineteen years, adults still need to design the curriculum based on what a total lifetime perspective says an educated person needs to know, needs to be able to do, and needs to be able to learn. Students will confidently and willingly follow the enthusiastic leadership plus the fascinating teaching of teachers who enable their students to fully become extreme students.

Extreme teachers cause extreme learning as they create, develop, nurture, challenge, and encourage extreme students. That adventure is forever new, forever important, forever meaningful, forever rewarding, and forever unlimited.

Chapter 9

Extreme Students and Their Families

Mr. and Mrs. Johnson noted that their children became quite interested in basketball and soccer at very young ages. Tasha would eagerly kick a soccer ball soon after she could walk. One of Shawn's early physical activities was to pick up a ball and throw it toward a trash can. As the toddlers grew into healthy children these interests, natural talents, and enjoyable activities were encouraged. Kimberly Johnson, the oldest of the three Johnson children, loved being older sister to Tasha and Shawn. She often challenged her younger brother and sister to a soccer match or a basketball game. When Kim was twelve she went to several sports camps and eagerly came home to teach Tasha, eight years old and Shawn, seven years old, everything she had learned.

Mr. and Mrs. Johnson entered the activities often. Backyard soccer matches or driveway basketball games were common activities for this family. If the weather allowed, two or more of the Johnson family members could usually be found outside playing basketball or soccer together. Some family vacations became basketball and soccer trips to watch professional teams compete. Some years the Johnson family put their vacation savings account toward sports camps for the children to attend. When Kimberly was sixteen, she played a major roll in her high school girls' soccer team being the runner-up in the state tournament. That same year Tasha's eleven- and twelve-year-old soccer team was undefeated and Shawn's fifth-sixth grade basketball team lost only one game. The local newspaper featured a long story about the Johnson family dynasty in local sports.

Kimberly began running on the track team her sophomore year in high school. The purpose was to improve her conditioning for soccer, but one unexpected result was her consistently high placement in track meet results. The one mile run was her best event. The outdoor soccer season, indoor soccer season, track season, and summer soccer camps filled the year with twelve months of sports. As a high school junior she was noticed by several college soccer coaches. As a high school senior, she was given five college athletic scholarship offers. The Johnson family vacation the summer after Kimberly's junior year of high school was a trek to visit colleges, which took them throughout several wonderful parts of the country.

Tasha continued to play soccer in youth leagues and at her middle school. High school rules allowed her to play on the junior varsity team of the high school she would attend. As an eighth grader she was the leading scorer for the high school junior varsity team.

Shawn's basketball skills were increasing and improving with extraordinary precision and acclaim. He was invited to present dribbling and shooting exhibitions at half-time of some local high school basketball games. One local college invited Shawn to present an identical half-time show at a postseason college basketball tournament game. That game was televised, and within a few days of the broadcast Shawn had been invited to be a guest on two national television programs.

Kimberly's college soccer career began with spectacular results but almost was limited to one season. She barely maintained academic eligibility during the soccer season as a freshman in college. During the second semester of college her grades dropped so much that she became convinced that she would fail several classes. She was placed on academic probation and became academically ineligible for her sophomore year. What went wrong?

As Kimberly struggled with college, Tasha and Shawn had some difficulties in high school. Middle school had been easy for both of them. Making a C in any class at their middle school was available to most any student who did the day-to-day work in class, paid any attention in class, and kept up with most of the homework. Tasha and Shawn both got in trouble for cheating. Tasha had another student write an English paper for her in tenth grade language arts class. Shawn used some material from the Internet as his own work in a ninth grade biology class. The resulting punishments were swift and effective. Tasha was removed from the soccer team for two weeks and required to attend Saturday school during those two weeks. Shawn was removed from the basketball team for two weeks and was given service work to do after school each day of those two weeks. He spent one hour after school as an assistant to the school's head custodian.

Mr. and Mrs. Johnson coped with these unprecedented family difficulties. What had gone wrong? They were very honest with each other. They wisely sought, accepted, and applied advice from counselors, teachers, and administrators at the high school Tasha and Shawn attended. They sought similar advice from the dean of Kimberly's college. During Christmas vacation after this very difficult first semester of Kimberly's sophomore year of college, Tasha's sophomore year of high school, and Shawn's freshman year of high school, the Johnson family took a completely different kind of trip. No sports games, no sports camps, no sports tournaments, and no sports activity of any kind were included.

This trip took the Johnsons to amazing museums, to the most technologically sophisticated libraries, to a symphony orchestra performance, to a church choir presentation of Handel's *Messiah* and to a New Year's Day symposium on personal excellence sponsored by several schools, health agencies, churches, businesses, and community groups in the Johnsons' hometown.

The emphasis of this trip was learning. Mr. and Mrs. Johnson had always been deeply devoted to their children. They now realized that their devotion, if measured in how time, money, and other family resources had been allocated, sent the message that the top family priority was athletics. The children understood that achievement in sports was the highest goal to set and the most important goal to reach.

The Johnsons continued to encourage athletic accomplishment. Kimberly became academically eligible again and by her junior year in college was on the dean's list. She also was the soccer team's leading scorer.

Tasha and Shawn never cheated again. They went to two academic camps in the summer and to two sports camps. They did volunteer work in the community. They won many soccer and basketball games. They continued to visit museums and libraries with their parents. They watched very few programs or sports events on television because Mr. and Mrs. Johnson had two reading lists uniquely developed for Tasha and for Shawn. As long as there were good books to read, television was an occasional reward, not a constant thief of otherwise productive time.

Mr. and Mrs. Johnson added a new learning experience for their children to build new academic skills through connections with the athletic talents and interests of Kimberly, Tasha, and Shawn. Each competitive athletic game or match would be followed by a written analysis of the event. The analysis could emphasize statistics as a way to explain a win or a loss, a good performance or a bad performance. The analysis could be an essay that described and evaluated the game or match. The analysis could be done through research that would include comments and observations from coaches, players, and spectators.

Shawn usually selected the statistical approach. One game in particular intrigued him. Shawn's team won the game 62-58. Shawn's basketball team was outscored in three-point shots by six points and in two-point shots by two points, but Shawn's team was nearly perfect from the free throw line hitting nineteen of twenty free throws and outscoring the other team in free throw points 19-7. The other team was seven for seventeen in free throw shooting. Shawn realized that the other team could have won the game if they had been twelve for seventeen from the free throw line. Shawn began doing some sophisticated statistical analysis of high school basketball games. He was amazed to discover how many games were decided by free throws. He began practicing free throws much more seriously. He had never thought that math was important in basketball, but he now saw basketball math as a real advantage in his quest to become a better basketball player.

Kimberly and Tasha often compared their soccer statistics and descriptions of what made the difference in many soccer matches. They knew how important it was to take good shots, defend or limit shots by the other team, always score on a penalty kick, or avoid getting a serious rule violation. Their written descriptions of soccer matches emphasized the importance of aggressive defense. They realized that their teams almost always won when they kept the other team to one or two goals in a game. They also realized that their teams won much more often when they played unselfishly, made great passes so a teammate could take a shot, and avoided serious rule violations that could result in a player having to leave the game temporarily or for the rest of the game.

Kimberly, Tasha, and Shawn had been reluctant to do these writing tasks, but they accepted the fact that it was required. They did not expect to learn anything from these sports essays and evaluations. They just did them at first to stay out of trouble and to be allowed to keep playing. They had to admit that they were playing the best basketball and soccer of their lives because of the new knowledge and understanding they were gaining. The same skills of analyzing sports were becoming useful in school classes. Kimberly did a very complex sports statistics project for a college probability and statistics class. Tasha wrote an A+ short story about a soccer team for her English class. Shawn designed a science project about what type of kicking method causes a soccer ball to go straight or to bend in an arc. The harmony of sports and school made the Johnson students more successful in their academic work and in their athletic efforts.

On those occasions when the Johnson family did watch a sporting event on television, everyone who watched wrote a quick analysis of the game and then their various ideas were discussed. This family time became one of the Johnson family's favorite traditions. They wondered if a sports television network might be interested in hiring the Johnson family to analyze sporting events and sports statistics.

Yes, this process took time and yes, there were a few complaints at first, but the complaints stopped quickly for two reasons. One, the parents made it explicitly clear that writing these evaluations of television sporting events was mandatory for all five family members. No excuses would be tolerated. Two, after writing the evaluations everyone read all of the evaluations. "I never thought of that" was heard during the first session of writing and then reading these analyses. Kimberly, Tasha, and Shawn had to admit that they were becoming more informed about and more knowledgeable about sports through this process. This family time together became enjoyable, meaningful, and productive.

�֍

Anne Harper had recently remarried after being divorced for three years. She and her first husband had one child, Jeremy, who was eleven years old. Jeremy's father moved to another town about a year ago. Anne's new husband, Chad Harper, had two children who lived with their mother. Jeremy misses his father a lot. Jeremy and Chad get along fairly well, but there are adjustments that have not been easy.

Jeremy has gotten in trouble a few times at school recently. His mother and teachers agreed that he was probably acting out frustration related to the divorce, to his father moving away, to his mother's remarriage, to a new stepfather, to a stepbrother and a stepsister who were strangers to him, and to the common ups and downs of middle school years.

Mrs. Harper took the advice of Jeremy's principal and visited school for one full day. She had always attended Jeremy's sporting events, music events, church events, and more throughout his life. She had volunteered at Jeremy's elementary school, but she just assumed that parents and guardians did not visit middle schools or high schools except for after school athletic events.

Her visit to Jeremy's sixth grade classes changed her thoughts about parental involvement. She observed that most students cooperated with teachers in classes. She also noticed two students whose only purpose seemed to be to disrupt everything in every class. Her son's education was being limited by the disorderly and defiant actions of those two eleven-year-old classroom criminals. Anne was surprised at how strongly her resentment toward those two students grew during the day. The teachers used every available, allowed, legal, ethical, and professional action to correct the misbehaviors. Nothing was completely effective. Jeremy later told his mother that one of the two students had already been arrested twice for crimes in the community and had been suspended from school often. The other student was in some special placement program in which federal and state laws or policies restricted teacher options so severely that unless a person spent endless hours reporting problems, reporting efforts made to solve the problems, and attending many meetings, nothing changed. Making all of that extra effort only to be told that the chronically disruptive, defiant, disorderly student had to stay in your classroom and learn from you while you also teach twenty-seven other students was one reason that some younger teachers in the school talked in the faculty lounge about finding a different career.

Anne Harper decided that what she had seen was unacceptable. Her employer agreed to her request for a flexible work schedule so she could visit school a half day each week. After three months of these regular visits, Anne compiled a complete summary of what she had observed. She had reached two major conclusions, which she presented to the school principal, the school district superintendent, and the school board. First, laws and policies need to include reasonable procedures for placing continuously disruptive, defiant, disorderly, and potentially dangerous students into alternative education programs that are in different locations than the standard school. Each middle school needs a full-time school law enforcement officer who patrols the school building, patrols the school campus, can process the investigation of some misbehaviors at school, investigates criminal misconduct at school, and works closely with the juvenile justice system as needed.

Anne's recommendations went nowhere at first. The principal, superintendent, and school board members thanked Anne for her time, concerns, and ideas. Anne was not satisfied. She worked with some elected officials in her state legislature to get formal consideration of her recommendations. Several newspaper reporters became interested in the persistence of one parent. The resulting newspaper stories generated much discussion. The state department of education established a task force on alternative education options and processes. Anne became a member of the task force. The school board authorized a committee to study how other school districts have implemented school law enforcement officer programs. Anne's husband, Chad, was named as a member of that committee. Anne and Chad knew that the task force and committee process would take time, would have no promise of desired results, and could be quite frustrating; however, there were problems that had to be confronted, issues that had to be raised, and solutions that had to be found. Their duties as parent and stepparent, as community members, as adults included being involved in schools.

⚜

Schools were closed due to an unexpected snow day. Kelly Walden's twin eight-year-old daughters needed to be taken care of today. Kelly's husband, David, was out of town on a three-day business trip. Kelly had several essential meetings with clients at her law firm's office. What to do? Call Nana. David's mother, a retired teacher, might be available to take care of the twins, Paula and Katie. A quick phone call to Nana and all of the plans were made. Kelly would take Katie and Paula to Nana's and pick them up after supper. Nana was delighted to spend the day with her granddaughters. Katie and Paula loved the idea of going to Nana's house, which is where their father lived during his childhood and teenage years.

Katie and Paula were surprised when Nana told them to keep their coats on. Why keep coats on inside Nana's house? Because they were going up to the attic to retrieve lots of papers and pictures from their father's years in elementary school, middle school, and high school. Their father's fortieth birthday was in two weeks. Nana's plan was for Katie, Paula, and Nana to each make a scrapbook for David Walden. Nana had kept everything from David's childhood—papers from school, tests and report cards from school, pictures and letters, everything. It was time to organize all of these items, which for years had filled filing cabinets. Making three scrapbooks—one for the elementary school years, one for the middle school years, and one for the high school years—was the project for this snow day.

Katie and Paula were very curious about their father. They asked hundreds of questions. They learned what their father liked and what he did when he was eight years old, their age. They wondered what it would have been like to be eight years old back then. Would they have been friends with David back then? They organized all of the files and the pictures by time period so each of the three scrapbooks would match with the sequential chronology of elementary, middle, and high school time periods. They read some of their father's school papers. They listened closely as Nana told the stories that went with each picture. It took only about thirty minutes of work in the attic to find the materials—artifacts as Nana called them—and to bring these many childhood and teenage souvenirs downstairs to set up the scrapbook-making work area on the large dining room table. The hours of this snow day passed quickly, enjoyably, and productively. Katie and Paula learned a lot about their father, about Nana, about other family members, about their hometown, and about themselves. This was an extremely good day. Grandmother and granddaughters learned together, listened to one another, thought much, explored curiosities, wondered, worked, interacted, organized materials and time, organized ideas and concepts, read, and created new memories. Nana's extreme teaching caused extreme learning in the lives of two dear extreme students, her granddaughters.

The experience that Nana provided for Katie and Paula appealed to the natural curiosity the girls had about their father's childhood. The research, reading, discussions, and scrapbooking work filled the snow day with learning, smiles, creativity, accomplishment, laughter, wonder, thinking, decision making, history, communication, analysis, evaluation, compare and contrast, fascination, questions, and joy. Each characteristic of extreme students was included in the scrapbook activity. Family projects can become extreme teaching, extreme learning, and extreme student endeavors if parents, guardians, grandparents, aunts, and uncles provide that structure. Some very normal and natural activities at or near home—cooking a meal, paying the bills, repairing a broken door handle, cleaning the basement, paying income taxes, going to the grocery store—can become learning experiences for children and teenagers if they are managed to include learning instead of merely completed to remove a chore from the daily to-do list.

No people are more fully informed about the wholesome knowledge, interests, and talents of children and teenagers than are their parents, guardians, or close relatives such as grandparents, aunts, and uncles. Those adults have known the child since birth. Those adults have shared experiences throughout the years in which personality emerged, interests developed, knowledge grew, talents were practiced, curiosities expanded, questions were asked perhaps relentlessly and repeatedly. Family members can plan, schedule, structure, and organize experiences that will help develop extreme student skills. "But this is a really cool television show and then I really need to play my video game" might be a common statement from a young person, but the adult needs to be the adult, limit the time given to passive activities, and involve himself or herself with the child in active and interactive learning experiences. The time together is priceless and cannot be retrieved, so make it count now. The mutual learning by the child about something new and by the adult about the child are wonderful returns on the investment of time together. When parents are extreme teachers who create an extreme learning home, the children and teenagers who live in such families are extreme students who have always understood the methods of, the adventures of, the benefits of, the work involved with, and the process of continuously living the characteristics, the life of extreme students.

EPILOGUE

"Congratulations, Andy, you have been an outstanding high school student. Your grades earned the number 3 rank in your class out of 378 graduates. You won many awards each year in high school. Your soccer team was the state champion your junior year. The school service work you did to provide new landscaping for the campus became an example of creativity, persistence, and environmental concerns. You've earned several highly valued college scholarship offers. Having taught you in two high school classes I know how dedicated, disciplined, and determined you are. As I've said at awards programs before, Andy, I want to be like you when I grow up. You have shown every student how to succeed and you've shown every teacher why our work is worth everything we put into it. Congratulations, Andy, on winning this year's Extreme Student Award."

What experiences from birth through high school graduation made Andy an extreme student? Family members, mentors, coaches, teachers, church youth leaders, Sunday school teachers, and neighbors interacted with Andy in ways that applied and developed his natural abilities while also guiding him in ways that helped create new skills. Andy's curiosities were nurtured. His questions were responded to seriously, yet sometimes with guidance, not answers, so he discovered answers instead of being told the answers. Andy's teachers appreciated his intellectual energy and challenged him to apply his thinking toward original, creative, difficult, rewarding tasks, projects, books, and papers. Andy's family showed him how to organize time and priorities as they organized family time and as they honored family priorities. Andy's family was not sympathetic to the "but why can't I watch television" or "everyone else gets to do that" when there were more important duties. Sure, Andy had plenty of enjoyable times, but he worked first and played later. Andy's family and teachers emphasized reading. His many interests in space exploration, sports, international travel, music, politics, and careers were matched with a supply of books, books, and more books to read on those topics. His family and his teachers would discuss the books with Andy after he read them. They paid attention to Andy's ideas and he paid attention to their questions, challenges, and encouragement.

Andy will remain an extreme student during college and throughout his life. The attitudes, skills, habits, and processes of being an extreme student are now fully incorporated into who Andy is and who he will become.

When asked to supply a quote for the school newspaper tribute to high school seniors edition, Andy thought for a moment and then spoke with a certain conviction. "Family members, teachers, and coaches have loved me throughout my life. My way of thanking them is to be the best Andy I can be, to live the most extremely complete life of honor and achievement that they challenged me and helped convince me to live."

Extreme teachers who cause extreme learning in the lives of children and teenagers get to be part of the adventure of developing, nurturing, challenging, rewarding, learning with, and learning from extreme students.

Appendix: Resources

Colleagues and graduate school students of mine often ask specific questions about what to do in specific situations. The materials in this appendix are included as answers to those questions and as inspiration for the creation of new answers to those questions.

I always survey middle school, high school, and graduate school students to identify what they already know and what topics they are eager to learn about. Those survey results, whenever possible, help shape the activities we do in class. This helps establish connections so school and real life are harmonious rather than separated. A survey is in the appendix.

My eighth grade economics students get excited about their homework projects. The samples of homework assignments will show why.

Designing materials for students to use that relate to real life and teach the required curriculum is efficient because more learning is caused and less reteaching is needed. Some math and science samples are enclosed.

The final pages in the appendix provide hope, inspiration, and some questions to ponder. This means that the book *Extreme Students* ends with the reader doing the thinking, the reflecting, the reading, the questioning, the curiosity exploring, and the mentally active thinking, the work that is part of being an extreme student.

In Class Survey:
Here's what I would like to know about money:
   1.

   2.

3.

4.

Here's what I would like to know about jobs and careers:
5.

6.

7.

8.

Here's what I would like to know about businesses:
9.

10.

11.

12.

Here's what I would like to know about legally and morally acquiring wealth:
13.

14.

15.

16.

Here's what I would like to know about how to avoid making mistakes with money, with jobs, with career, with shopping, with acquiring wealth:
17.

18.

19.

20.

There's one other economic question or idea I need to know more about:
21.

In Class Project:

1. Based on our November 15, 2004 survey of your favorite cereals, these were mentioned:

Cap'n Crunch Peanut Butter	Original Cap'n Crunch
Cap'n Crunch Berries	Frosted Flakes
Special K with Strawberries	Honey Nut Cheerios
Cocoa Pebbles	Cocoa Puffs
Honeycomb	Waffle Crisp
Berry Berry Kix	Cinnamon Toast Crunch
Lucky Charms	Fruity Pebbles
Golden Grahams	Froot Loops

2. What economic conclusions can we reach from the results of our survey?

3. Breakfast cereals are not just for breakfast any more. For some consumers, cereal works for lunch, supper, snacks, and treats. Plus, the once upon a time limited choices of Corn Flakes, Rice Krispies, Shredded Wheat, and Oatmeal now are joined by 100 or so other options.

   What could a new cereal offer that would get grocery stores to put it on the shelves, would get consumers to try it, and would get consumers to keep purchasing it?

   Think about a target market . . . which means the people for whom a product is designed. Example: Shredded Wheat is designed to appeal to a different group of consumers than Cinnamon Toast Crunch is or than Froot Loops is. The advertising used is different—what media are used and what/how the message is communicated. Maybe you advertise Shredded Wheat on the NBC *Today* program and Froot Loops on a Saturday morning cartoon program.

4. ADVENTURE, CHALLENGE, OPPORTUNITY, AND WORK:

   Work in groups of 3 to 5 students to invent a new cereal that has a "unique selling proposition," meaning it is different in at least one important way from its competition.

   To identify the target market for the cereal and to be sure that the product provides benefits for that group of people.

   To design the package to enhance the appeal of the product and the presentation of the product.

To create and to present a commercial for the product.

To create a way to get a "trial" of the product . . . meaning to make it very easy for people to taste/try our new product.

Ready, set . . . think, think more, keep thinking, and then complete the adventure, challenge, opportunity, and work.

Homework:

Due: Friday, October 29, 2004, 9:37 a.m. eastern standard time—results, not excuses, which means in this case, "I don't have it" is unacceptable.

1. Write a story that is about economics and that includes all of the "core content" vocabulary terms about economics. Underline each of the terms when they are used in your story.

2. Make a set of flash cards with one card for each of the "core content" vocabulary terms about economics. On one side is the vocabulary term. On the other side is (A) the definition and (B) a picture or a drawing that shows the meaning of, idea of, and/or example of the term.

3. Create a card game, a board game, or a video game that uses all of the "core content" vocabulary for economics. For a card game or a board game, actually make the game. For a video game, you could use drawings ("storyboards" they are called in advertising) to show the pictures which would become the video . . . or you may have a better idea.

The project I'm going to do is _____

My first ideas for the project are _____
_____
_____

To make sure that I complete this project on time and to do this project very well I need to _____
_____

To prevent any problems with completing this project on time and very well I need to _____
_____
_____

Homework:

Due: Friday, November 12, 2004, 9:37 a.m. eastern standard time—results, not excuses

1. Invent a new car that will be sold beginning in October 2006.

   a. Give the car a name and tell why that is the best name for this car.

   b. Write the 30-second radio commercial for the car. Tell consumers what is unique and what is better about this car.

   c. Write the script for and draw 3 scenes from the video of a 30-second television commercial for the car.

   d. Design, on paper, the homepage of the website for the new car and include at least 6 links.

   e. Create a promotion that will motivate people to come to the car dealership and test-drive this car.

2. You decide to do with milk what Starbucks has done with coffee. Create the new store.

   a. Give the store name and tell why that is the best name for this store.

   b. Write the 30-second radio commercial for the store. Tell consumers what is unique and what is better about this store. Be sure to tell about the products available at the store.

   c. Write the script for and draw 3 scenes from the video of a 30-second television commercial for the store.

   d. Design, on paper, the homepage of the website for the new store and include at least 6 links.

   e. Create a promotion that will motivate people to come to the new store and try your products.

3. Create a new radio station that is designed to appeal to middle school students and to high school students.

   a. Give the radio station its call letters and a nickname. Tell why this is the best nickname for this station.

b. Write the 30-second radio commercial for the station. Tell listeners what is unique and what is better about this station.

c. Write the script for and draw 3 scenes from the video of a 30-second television commercial for the new station.

d. Design, on paper, the homepage of the website for the new station and include at least 6 links.

e. Create a promotion that will motivate people to listen to the new station.

Homework:

Due: Friday, December 3, 2004, 9:37 a.m. eastern standard time.

1. Invent a new television program about economics.

a. What is the name of the television program?

b. Why is that the perfect name for the program?

c. What channel/network is it on?

d. Why is that the best channel/network for it to be on?

e. What time is the program on?

f. Why is that the best time for the program to be on?

g. What four topics would be included in the first episode of the program?

1.

2.

3.

4.

h. Draw a newspaper advertisement that tells people about this new program. Include the name of the program, the time it is on, channel/network it is on, what the program is about, and a contest that people who watch the first episode can enter.

i. A person who just opened a savings account with a new bank is interviewed on the program. Write two questions you would ask that person and give their answer.

1.

2.

Math Progress and Application:

3	5	7	2	6	8
+4	+3	+4	+8	+7	+1

3 cookies + 4 cookies =

5 cakes + 3 cakes =

7 pies + 4 pies =

2 pieces of pizza + 8 pieces of pizza =

6 bottles of water + 7 bottles of water =

8 candy bars + 1 candy bar =

I have 3 cookies and you have 4 cookies. Who has more cookies?

One teacher baked 5 cakes and another teacher baked 3 cakes. How many cakes are there?

One family brought 7 pies to the school picnic. Another family brought 4 pies to the school picnic. How many pies are there at the picnic? _____ If each pie provides 8 slices, how many slices are there? _____

A student ate 2 pieces of pizza. Another pizza had 8 slices and 4 other students ate all of those slices with each student eating the same number of pieces. How many total pieces of pizza were eaten? _____ How many slices did each student eat? _____

You buy 6 bottles of water. You then buy 6 more and get one free. How many total bottles of water do you have?

You have 8 candy bars and then a friend gives you another candy bar. How many candy bars do you have?

Each cookie costs 25 cents. How much will 7 cookies cost?

Each cake costs $8. How much will 8 cakes cost?

Each pie costs $6. How much will 11 pies cost?

Pizza is $1.25 per slice. How much will 10 slices cost?

Water is $1 per bottle. Buy 12 get one free. How much will 13 bottles cost?

Candy bars are 4 for $1. How much will 9 candy bars cost?

3 cookies have 300 calories. How many calories would 4 cookies have?

8 cakes are cut into 20 pieces per cake. How many total pieces of cake are there?

11 pies are divided into peach pie, chocolate pie, and strawberry pie. There are 3 peach pies. There are as many chocolate pies as there are strawberry pies. How many chocolate pies are there? How many strawberry pies are there?

How could two pizzas that are exactly the same size be sliced so 2 pieces of one pizza would equal the amount of pizza in 8 slices of the other pizza?

13 bottles of water are poured into two pitchers to exactly fill the pitchers. How many bottles went into each pitcher?

You bought 9 candy bars for 25 cents each. How much did you spend? A friend offers to buy 5 of your candy bars for 40 cents each. If you sell the 5 candy bars, how much money will you get? Is this a good deal for you or not? Explain three reasons why you would or would not sell the 5 candy bars for 40 cents each.

Space: For Elementary School, Middle School, and High School

1. Thoughts of a second grade student who gazes up at the stars. Questions that student might ask. Big ideas that student might have. Adventures that student might imagine. Dreams that student might dream.

2. Thoughts of a sixth grade student who gazes up at the stars. Questions that student might ask. Big ideas that student might have. Adventures that student might imagine. Dreams that student might dream. Topics that student could consider for a science fair project related to space.

3. Thoughts of an eleventh grade student who gazes up at the stars through a sophisticated telescope at a university his/her physics class visited. Questions that student might ask. Big ideas that student might have. College majors that student might consider as inspired by this field trip. Career interests that student might consider as inspired by this field trip. Research that student could do for a paper or an experiment for physics class.

Dear Extreme Teacher,

Hope.

I hope that you have a wonderful week with your students.

I hope that there are many moments of joy, of inspiration, of accomplishment, of peace, and of, well, of hope itself.

Hope . . . to know that despite difficulties of the moment, there is still beauty and goodness nearby and within.

Hope . . . to recall fears that were overcome, to gain strength from difficulties that were mastered, and to gain faith from the wonder of another sunrise giving mankind a heavenly signal of eternal hope.

What comes to your mind when you think of hope?

Teachers are people of hope. We hope that all students will learn. We hope that our colleagues will be dedicated and helpful. We hope that weekends will be long enough to provide recovery from the past week, preparation for the next week, and some completely random or some perfectly planned adventures which are good for heart, mind, body, and soul.

I hope that today is a wonderful day for you. I hope that you and your students create extreme learning. I hope that your day is filled with smiles and ideas, with success and with goodness, with proper challenges that enable you to discover new levels of your own greatness.

Success, Communication, and Hope

Finally I get to do something interesting at school. I hate this place. I, Shawn Cooper, really hate this place. Is it OK if I just keep writing I hate this place, I hate this place, I hate this place. I mean, come on, this is school. Everyone hates school. School is boring. The work we have to do is just, well, it's just so nothing. Who cares about math and science? Who cares about what farmers grow in Asia and what the Spanish word for hello is?

How's that for an introduction to this stupid paper I have to write for my stupid sophomore English class. It's OK to say stupid, right, because you said it could express my opinion, so that's my opinion. This paper is stupid. This class is stupid. The teacher, well, you are actually OK because you are not exactly like most other teachers I've had, but you still make me do work and I refuse to do any work. The only reason I am writing this paper is because you said I could write about absolutely anything including why it is so stupid to write a paper so that's what I am writing about. Why writing a paper is stupid.

First, writing this paper is stupid because nobody writes anything any more. We send e-mail. We send instant messages. We text message. We use cell phones. Right after Christmas my mother asked me if I was going to write thank you notes to people who gave me a present for Christmas. Huh. Thank you what? Notes. Nobody writes notes. That was from another century. I told her I would call people to say thinks, so I did and that really meant leaving messages on voice mail. No big deal. But, come on, writing notes and putting a stamp on them and going to the post office. Yeah and then I'm going to listen to my favorite music on my record player or maybe on my 8-track tape players. After that I'll play my newest, favorite video game—Pac Man. Get real.

Second, this paper is on paper. Come one, electronic is what works now. Why not let me send this to you with e-mail. I still would not want to do it and I probably would not do it, but if you let me do my work electronically, who knows, maybe one night I would be really bored at home and I could just type something and send it to you. The fun would be that you got e-mail from me. Imagine sending e-mail to my teacher. It sure beats handing you a piece of paper. Save a tree would ya. Skip the paper.

Third, this paper is for school and I hate school and I hate school and I hate school. I refuse to work and I refuse to work and I refuse to work. My 6th grade teacher would tell me that those were run-on sentences and she would be right. Is it illegal to have a run-on sentence? At least it is a sentence, right?

Fourth, this paper is stupid because the time I am taking in the school computer lab to type and then to print this paper could have been spent talking to Becky about the concert we are going to this Friday night. It will be so cool. And guess what? The band at the concert will not ask me to write a paper about the concert.

So, don't expect me to do any more work because I've just finished the only paper I intend to write and I wrote it because the subject was the only one that has ever made sense to me in all the years I was in school and was told to write a paper. Finally, I got to tell a teacher what I think of writing papers. The end.

"Hi, this is Ms. Roberts from Centertown High School. May I speak with Ms. Cooper, please?"

"This is Ms. Cooper and I cannot believe you are calling again. I get so many calls from Shawn's school. Sometimes it is that automatic machine you have that calls to tell me about some fund-raiser at the school. Or I get a call from the assistant principal telling me that Shawn skipped class. I know he skips. What am I supposed to do? I work. I work at a big office of a giant company. I work in information technology. Computers all day. They break and I fix them. The system goes down and I get it back up. People complain to me all day, every day. People are never satisfied. We are changing out a lot of old computers for new computers. Guess who has to do all of that? Right, me. I also have to find something to do with the old computers. I have that job and I actually have two jobs because I do some computer teaching work on my own. Grown-ups who know nothing about computers ask me to teach them. Shawn's stepfather works full time and then some overtime. I can't keep up with all of the calls from the school and everything else I have to do."

"I just wanted to tell you . . . "

"I know what you wanted to tell me. Shawn says that book was stolen from his locker. The book costs $57. How can I pay for that? It was stolen. What's wrong with the lockers at your school? He should not have to pay for a book that was stolen."

"Well, for my class he has his book, in fact he . . . "

"He got in trouble, right? I guess he called you some awful name. Well, can't you control him? Don't you have some system to deal with that or am I supposed to do everything?"

"Ms. Cooper, Shawn made an A grade in my class. He made an A. That's what I've been trying to tell you."

A moment of silence. "I knew he could do it. My boy made an A. How about that? What did you say your name is?"

"My name is Katie Roberts. I teach English at Shawn's high school. He wrote a really amazing paper. He probably thinks he flunked it, but he made an A. The whole idea of the paper was to express an opinion that the student really feels strongly about. He wrote about how much he hated having to write the paper. Can you believe that? He wrote a great paper about how much he hates having to write a paper. He really expressed strong ideas. I'll show him how to correct the writing process, but all I was after was a strong opinion, you know, just show some real feeling, take a stand, think. He did all of that. I wanted you to know how well he did."

"Thanks. You know, thanks. I can't remember ever getting a call like that. Hey, about that book. We'll look around the house. Maybe it is here."

"I'll talk to Shawn about the book and see what class it is from and maybe we can look at school, too. Please feel free to call me when I can be of help. Feel free to visit school whenever you would like to meet with me or just see what is going on here."

"Thanks. Thanks a lot. I think I'll go tell Shawn that his English teacher called. Imagine what he will think of that. Hey, is there something I could do for you or for your school?"

"Well, are any of those old computers available for a donation to the school?

"Hi. Ms. Roberts. My mom told me you called. She said that I made an A on the paper I wrote. I still think it is a stupid paper and it was a stupid assignment. But, you know what happened? I get to go take my driver's license permit test because I made an A. I've been 16 years old for two months, but I was not allowed to take that test because I cause so many problems at school. Mom asked me what I wanted for making the A. I told her I wanted to take my permit test. She said I could. It's still a stupid paper, but if that's what it takes to get my driving permit, it was worth it. I still hate school. I still think that's a stupid paper. How in the world did I get an A on the paper anyway? And what did you mean by the comment you made when you glanced at my paper that you were going to a concert this Friday and you wondered what kind of music I like?

Optimistic? Yes, maybe outrageously.

Possible? Yes, very possible right here, right now.

How?

Will it work every time? No.

So why try? Read School Thought 1 from *Extreme Teaching.*

Now, why try?

What's the big idea of "Success, Communication, and Hope?"

Graduate School Class—Exam Questions:

1. It's just too much. Some of my students are so capable. They could skip a grade or a class or more. They deserve to be challenged, but I have other students who are behind grade level, who have little motivation and who, well, who just don't care, then there are students who care, who try, and who barely pass. I'm one teacher with all of those levels of achievement in my classroom all day, day after day, each group of students has some version of this. What am I supposed to do?

   Write your answer to this sincere question from a colleague. Make any adjustments so the question applies directly to the level of education you work with—elementary, middle, or high school—and to the subject(s) you work with. Apply some of the discussion, activities and readings from class, plus your experience and judgment.

2. Two teachers in the faculty lounge during lunch were talking. "What we teach our students now is so much like what I was taught when I was in school. Why do we keep the old curriculum? Even with state reforms of education and with other changes, the subjects are still the same old subjects. Don't we need to update what we teach?"

"I agree. Plus, some of the teaching methods used now are, just like you said about subjects, the same old methods. Don't students in 2004 need some different ways of learning. Not that all of the old ways have to be discarded, but come on, we know so much about how to teach, about how the brain works and what great teachers do. Our school council needs to have some committee look into this. Well, not much time left for our duty free lunch. At least it is duty free, but it is still a time to think. Something has to change."

Think of the curriculum at your school—what is taught and how it is taught—in terms of what these two teachers from your school said. Assume that their perspectives are valid and merit some response. What actions would you suggest in response to their thoughts? Apply some of the discussions, activities, and readings from class, plus your experience and judgment.

Making Education Real, Fascinating, and Personal

Five years ago I was asked by Jim Thomas, the principal of the school where I am the associate principal, if I would like to teach a class at our school in addition to my duties as an administrator. Having been reared by parents and grandparents who insisted on good manners and having been born to teach, I eagerly said, "Yes, sir!" Five years later the teaching adventure continues to fascinate me as students and I learn together.

During the October through December 2004 quarter of the school year I taught eighth grade Economics. The results show that every student in the class made an "A" or "B" grade. There was no achievement gap. Every student turned in every homework project. The projects were done with masterful creativity. When homework assignments were given to the students their response was always one of eagerness, of excitement, and of willingness. Tests were used occasionally when that was the best way to teach. Tests measured and applied the students' strong achievement. Tests also measured my effectiveness and showed me what corrections to make in my teaching.

Despite what some critics may say, impressive learning takes place hour by hour, classroom by classroom throughout much of Kentucky according to many quantifiable measures and according to many of my colleagues. Thorough research which I have done for the past eight years confirms that we know what great teachers do to cause that impressive learning. There are four characteristics of great teachers according to that research: (1) great teachers use a variety of teaching methods and activities; (2) great teachers challenge their students; (3) great teachers are enthusiastic about teaching, about learning, about students; and (4) great teachers connect learning today with the real lives of students today.

A more concise summary is in these words: real, fascinating, personal. When learning experiences at school are real, are fascinating, and are personalized, students will eagerly commit to doing the work. Textbooks and worksheets—commonly used materials in many classrooms—can help serve a basic, limited purpose, but they are not real, fascinating, or personal. An Economics activity in which students create a new brand of breakfast cereal, design the package, create the website, write a commercial, and show how the new product connects with economic terminology such as profit, competition, opportunity cost, supply and demand, technology, capital, risk, and advertisement can be very real for students, can fascinate students, can be personalized by students, and can cause learning.

Recent news articles and reports have expressed concerns about limited progress made in Kentucky's education system and made nationally in schools. In an honorable search for the perfect system, law, policy, or bureaucratic organization, recommendations will emerge to reform the most recent education reform. Some of those recommendations will have merit and could help. Others may just be a distraction, may just create a mountain of new paperwork, and may, at worst, create new problems. We know what works in education and it is not dependent upon bureaucratic reform or a further increase in the federal government's role in education. The ultimate reform of education is great teaching. In Fayette County, Kentucky, there are many great teachers who daily dedicate themselves to students. Also, in Fayette County there are many great students who daily dedicate themselves to academic success. Those people know what works in education. Listening closely to those great teachers and to those great students could provide ideas that are less costly and more effective than some adjustments in bureaucratic structures or public law.

The Prichard Committee for Academic Excellence and the Fayette County Public Schools recently held an important public forum about education. Most Fayette County and Central Kentucky members of the Kentucky legislature attended the forum along with parents, guardians, educators, and community members. Concerns, ideas, and convictions were expressed honestly and honorably at that forum. Here's one idea to add to that discussion and to the overall current attention given to education:

When the topic of education is discussed in terms of public policy or in terms of a state budget, in terms of national priorities or in terms of government reorganization to better provide public services, please remember Tasha and Shawn. Who are Tasha and Shawn? They are students and they are real people, living real lives, right now. When the state budget is debated, the money for Tasha's new math book gets included in a line of the budget for instructional materials. When those funds are reduced to zero for a year, as happened recently, it is not just a line in the budget that is changed, it is a new math book or other new instructional supplies which Tasha will not get to use. When school technology funds are seen as lines on a budget it can seem rather impersonal, but when those funds are seen as a new computer for Shawn to use, it can mean more. Tasha and Shawn will not be in Frankfort when the General Assembly meets. They will be in school using old math books and old computers hoping that Kentucky's leaders will make a personal vow to Tasha and Shawn to find a way to provide what is needed to equip Tasha's classroom and Shawn's school computer lab.

"No Child Left Behind" is a rather general statement. I would encourage local, state, and national leaders to put a name and a face with the statement. Come visit our schools to meet Tasha and Shawn. Come be a substitute teacher for a few days so you can work with Tasha and Shawn. Then, when you return to local, state, or national legislative sessions the effort will not be for the generic concept of education, but for the very real, very personal content of Tasha's education and of Shawn's education.

Tasha and Shawn are real, fascinating, and personal. They thrive on real, fascinating, and personal educational activities in classrooms. Teachers who make education real, fascinating, and personal will see Tasha and Shawn do great work, will cause learning, and will learn with and from Tasha and Shawn.

Political leaders who make education policy decisions based on a knowledge of and a vow to Tasha and Shawn will find a way to provide the necessary support. Education is best when it is real, fascinating, and personal. Challenges of limited budgets, competition of different political agendas, the nature of bureaucracies, and the complex process of improving public policies combine to present a demanding task. That task may be more difficult than it is fascinating, but if people involved in the bold battle for better schools will think of and work with parents/guardians, community members, students, and educators in real and personal ways, Kentucky, other states, and local communities could see some unprecedented progress in classroom and in schools.

Education is about Tasha and Shawn. A personal and a real commitment to Tasha and to Shawn could honorably obligate us and could persistently inspire us to find a way to make education real, fascinating, and personal. There will always be political debates. Agreement on providing the best possible education for Tasha and Shawn could enable Kentucky to rise above the limitations of the past and to build upon a new, unbridled spirit of educational teamwork, achievement, and results.

Index

About the Author

Keen J. Babbage has taught social studies in grades 7 through 12 and education classes at the college and graduate levels. He has school administration experience with grades 6 through 12 and has executive experience with three large corporations. He is the author of *911: The School Administrator's Guide to Crisis Management* (ScarecrowEducation, 1996), *Meetings for School-Based Decision Making* (ScarecrowEducation, 1997), *High-Impact Teaching: Overcoming Student Apathy* (ScarecrowEducation, 1998), *Extreme Teaching* (ScarecrowEducation, 2002), and *Extreme Learning* (ScarecrowEducation, 2004).